HUMAN ORIGINS

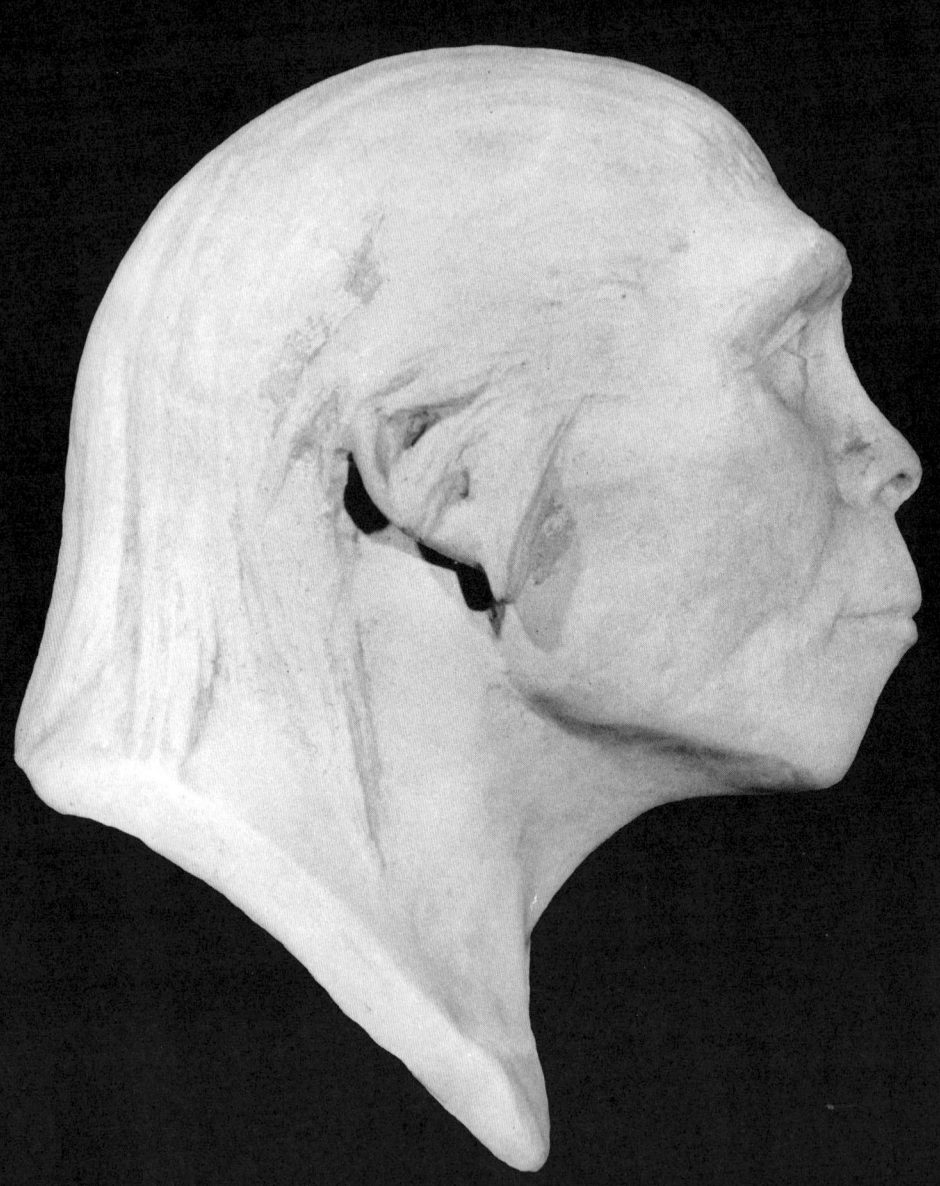

Sculptor's conception of *Homo erectus* female.
Courtesy of *Douglas H. Smith*.

THOMAS W. MC KERN and SHARON MC KERN

The University of Kansas

HUMAN ORIGINS

An Introduction to Physical Anthropology

PRENTICE-HALL, INC., Englewood Cliffs, New Jersey

© 1969 by PRENTICE-HALL, INC.
ENGLEWOOD CLIFFS, NEW JERSEY

All rights reserved.
No part of this book may be reproduced
in any form or by any means without
permission in writing from the publisher

Current printing (last digit):
10   9   8   7   6   5   4   3   2   1

C-13-445221-6
P-13-445213-5

Library of Congress catalog card number
74–87970

Printed in the United States of America

Prentice-Hall International, Inc., *London*
Prentice-Hall of Australia, Pty. Ltd., *Sydney*
Prentice-Hall of Canada, Ltd., *Toronto*
Prentice-Hall of India Private Ltd., *New Delhi*
Prentice-Hall of Japan, Inc., *Tokyo*

FOR HAP
with deep affection

PREFACE

The present book is designed to serve as an introduction to physical anthropology. The books beside it on the bookshelf will have more pages and longer bibliographies, and, perhaps, grander illustrations, for this volume is meant to be a *little* book. It is meant also to be used in association with, rather than instead of, its larger literary relatives.

Physical anthropology is a wide and complex science. The trend in textbooks published for students, both academic and lay, has been to emphasize such topics as the complexities of taxonomy and the mechanistic intricacies of blood chemistry and molecular genetics. These and others represent real and crucial problems within the scope of physical anthropology and they must be considered at length, ideally in those larger books and in the classroom. But what of the liberal arts student who elects to take a brief survey course in human origins, or the layman who hopes to become better informed, or the junior college student who sees the new inclusion of physical anthropology courses in his curriculum?

To the present authors, it seems both unnecessary and unwise to bludgeon the typical introductory student with a maze of technical knowledge. We feel the time has come rather to educate and stimulate the student whose only motivation for sampling this science is his natural curiosity for an area about which he knows little. He may go no further, in which case we are gratified that he rests with a basic knowledge of the nature of man; or he may use this little book to build a framework of inquiry, seeking answers in larger books and more advanced courses, in which case we are more than gratified to have sent him on his way.

This is not to say that a little book by virtue of its size evades the larger issues. It simply condenses them, presenting those issues in careful definition, while striving to impart the fundamental facts and problems involved *at an introductory level*. Emphasis has been placed on what the authors consider a logical organization, and technical details are generalized, though guides to those details in other works are given. In this way, we hope, the little book will induce its readers to ask big questions.

It takes a lot of people to produce even the smallest volume, and the authors are grateful for the cooperation and assistance of many; among them are Mr. Douglas H. Smith, for his photography of fossil man casts; Dr. William R. Maples, University of Texas, for original primate photographs; Dr. Bertram Kraus and Harper & Row for permission to reprint; Dr. Robert Squier and Dr. William Bass, University of Kansas, for constant encouragement; Mr. Larry Quade, University of Kansas, for manuscript preparation. Special thanks for help of another and more personal nature go to Dr. Richard Brooks and Dr. Sheilagh Brooks, Nevada Southern University; to Mrs. Jeanette Smith and Mrs. Rosa McPhail of Austin, Texas; and to Dr. and Mrs. W. C. McKern of Berkeley, California.

T. W. McK.

S. McK.

Lawrence, Kansas

CONTENTS

Chapter   **INTRODUCTION**   2
1   The Social Sciences *3,* The Study of Man *4,* Subdivisions of Anthropology *4,* History of Anthropology *5,* Scope of Physical Anthropology *6,* **Suggested Readings**   7

Chapter   **MAN IN NATURE**   8
2   Classification *10,* Typological Approach *11,* Phylogenetic Approach *11,* Similarities: Analogous and Homologous *12,* The Classification of Man *13,* **Suggested Readings**   19

Chapter   **EVOLUTION—IN THEORY**   20
3   Catastrophism *22,* Developmental Theory *22,* Darwin's Theory of Evolution *24,* Lamarck: Acquired Characteristics *25,* Weissmann: Continuity of the Germ Plasm *26,* Mendel: The Laws of Heredity *26,* Man and Evolution *30,* **Suggested Readings**   31

Chapter	32 EVOLUTION—IN FACT
4	Comparative Anatomy *34,* Embryology *35,* Geography *37,* Serology *39,* Paleontology *41,* Genetics *42,* **Suggested Readings** *43*

Chapter	44 GEOLOGIC TIME
5	Law of Superposition *46,* Fossils and Life History *48,* Faunal Succession *48,* Geologic Time Scale *49,* Geochronology *52,* Limitations of Radioactive-dating Methods *55,* **Suggested Readings** *57*

Chapter	58 THE FOSSIL PRIMATES
6	Orthogenesis *59,* Developmental Trends Among the Primates *60,* The Fossil Primates *64,* Fossils of the Paleocene *65,* Fossils of the Eocene *66,* Fossils of the Oligocene *67,* Fossils of the Miocene and Pliocene *68,* Summary *72,* **Suggested Readings** *73*

Chapter	74 FOSSIL MAN
7	Nomenclature Systems *76,* Differentiation of Hominids and Pongids *77,* The *Australopithecines* *79,* Problem Cases *81, Homo erectus 84, Homo sapiens neanderthalensis 88,* Problem Cases *94, Homo sapiens sapiens 98,* Conclusion *100,* **Suggested Readings** *101*

Chapter	102 CULTURAL PREHISTORY
8	Culture and Human Behavior *103,* Divisions of the Paleolithic *106,* The Lower Paleolithic *107,* The Middle Paleolithic *111,* The Upper Paleolithic *114,* The New World *119,* **Suggested Readings** *123*

Chapter	124 PRIMATOLOGY
9	Methods of Investigation *125,* The Howler Monkey *129,* The Baboon *131,* The Gibbon *134,* The Orangutan *136,* The Gorilla *136,* The Chimpanzee *138,* **Suggested Readings** *142*

xi   Contents

Chapter **HEREDITY** *144*
10
Applications of Genetics *145*, Cellular Reproduction *146*, The Physical Bases of Heredity *147*, Mitosis *148*, Meiosis *152*, Sex Determination *153*, Dominance *156*, Genotype-Phenotype *157*, Sex Linkage *158*, Mutations *160*, Populations and Gene Pools *162*, **Suggested Readings** **163**

Chapter **HUMAN VARIATION** *164*
11
Studies with Comparative Populations *166*, Tools in Human Variation *167*, Anthropometry *167*, Skin Color or Pigmentation *169*, Hair Color *170*, Eye Pigmentation *170*, Hair Form *171*, Eye Form *171*, Dentition *171*, Blood Types *172*, **Suggested Readings** **177**

Chapter **RACE** *178*
12
A Racial Taxonomy *182*, **Suggested Readings** **187**

Chapter **ANTHROPOLOGY: TODAY AND TOMORROW** *188*
13
The Continued Refinement of Research Tools *190*, Outside the Laboratory *190*, Twentieth-Century Trends *191*, Future Man *193*, **Suggested Readings** **197**

INDEX *198*

HUMAN ORIGINS

INTRODUCTION

chapter
1

It is both customary and wise, when introducing any field of inquiry, for the authors to begin with a definition of the study itself. In the case of human origins, the problem dealt with specifically by a young and ambitious science termed *physical anthropology,* it is helpful to begin at an even more elemental level. Thus the initial question is not "What is the study of man?" but rather "What is man?"

Man is first of all a biological entity, subject to the same natural laws as other animals. His uniqueness lies in his capacity for culture—that potential, derived from a mental development unsurpassed by the remainder of the animal kingdom, which enables man to manipulate his environment to suit his own comfort and desires.

The Social Sciences

In a sense, all the sciences are concerned with man; they differ only in approach or emphasis. *Psychology,* for example, studies man from the viewpoint of individual human behavior. *Sociology* studies behavior within the human group. *History* approaches the study of man on the basis of past human events. *Economics* limits its inquiry to problems of human trade and exchange; *physiology* and *biochemistry* deal with the human body. All of these sciences share a common goal: an understanding of man. Each, however, selects a single aspect through which to approach and explore toward that understanding.

The Study of Man

Anthropology, on the other hand, prefers not to concentrate on any single aspect of man's nature, seeking instead to investigate man as a whole. Because man can be classified neither as a wholly biological nor as a wholly social animal, anthropology takes into account his dual nature, subjecting him to natural laws yet with constant reference to the ways in which he may modify or direct the course of his own destiny. The uniqueness of anthropology, then, lies in its concern with the totality of man. By definition, it is an infinitely complex science, which confronts and attempts to delineate the greatest problems of humanity in every area.

Subdivisions of Anthropology

Such complexity both invites and necessitates specialization, in order to make the subject more manageable for scientific investigation. Generally, anthropology is divided into two main categories: *cultural* and *physical anthropology.* The former concerns itself with the origins and history of man's culture, and may include such diverse subdivisions as:

1. *Archeology,* the study of evidence left by past cultures;
2. *Ethnography,* the descriptive study of human societies;
3. *Ethnology,* the science of peoples, their cultures, and their life histories as groups;
4. *Social anthropology,* the study of social structure (kinship, political organization, law, religion, and economic activities);
5. *Linguistics,* the study of written or spoken language.

Physical anthropology, the study of the development and present nature of man's physical structure, considers man first as a biological entity—always, however, with a view of his cultural capacities. Physical anthropology is subdivided into numerous fields of further specialization, among which are:

    1. *Somatology,* the study of organs and systems of the human body and their relationships;
    2. *Paleoanthropology,* the study of ancient fossil man;
    3. *Primatology,* the study of the primates related to man;
    4. *Osteology,* the study of the bone structure of man;
    5. *Anthropometry,* the study of the comparative measurement of human populations.

History of Anthropology

Physical anthropology, like anthropology in general, owes its beginnings to the late nineteenth-century scientists of Europe, who concerned themselves with such diverse fields of investigation as anatomy, geology, neurosurgery, and psychology. For example, the special knowledge of the anatomists concerning man's internal structure led to an interest in the comparative nature of world populations and to a consideration of man's relationship to the lower primates (apes and monkeys). As the early geologists began to establish fossil sequences through evidence found in the ancient earth layers, they had to include a number of fossil forms that were obviously the skeletal remains of man, representing human populations dating back many thousands of years. Thus a growing interest in the variability of living human populations, coupled with an awakening to the fact that man has an exceedingly long history on this earth, stimulated the birth of a new science, now termed *anthropology.*

The first official recognition of anthropology as a legitimate field of scientific inquiry came in 1859 with the establishment by Paul Broca of the Society of Anthropology in Paris, France. The members of the Society, many of whom were known and highly respected within their own professions, spent their time observing and recording the differences of world populations, both living and skeletal. Later, as human fossil evidence began to accumulate, these early pioneers of anthropology began to think in terms of evolutionary development.

A trend toward specialization and refinements in methodologies led to a recognition of anthropology with its present division into physical and cultural anthropology. This development can be considered a part of the natural growth of the science of man and attests to its place among the social sciences as an all-inclusive study of *Homo sapiens*.

Scope of Physical Anthropology

This book, while making constant reference to man's cultural potential, seeks to explore the specialized field of physical anthropology or, as it is sometimes called, *human biology*. From the viewpoint of the physical anthropologist, we will consider first man's place in nature, his taxonomic classification within the animal kingdom. We will discuss evolution in theory, as advanced by Darwin and other pioneers, and in fact, as shown by the evidence gleaned from studies in closely aligned sciences, such as comparative anatomy, embryology, geography, serology, paleontology, and genetics. Later, we will consider geologic time and the methods for dating remains of early life forms. We will concern ourselves in detail with fossil man and with probable fossil ancestors. Through investigations of primate behavior, we will hypothesize regarding the social life of early man.

In keeping with the total view of man, we will summarize cultural prehistory, sifting through the artifacts left behind by ancient man as clues to his development. And we will consider human variation: genetics, evolutionary mechanisms, race, blood groups in man and among the nonhuman primates, measurement of man, and skeletal identification. Ultimately we will question the ways in which physical anthropology applies its methodology to modern-day problems.

It will be seen, in exploring the areas noted above, that the physical anthropologist is dependent to a great extent upon information and techniques borrowed from other disciplines.

While many techniques with which to study man have been devised by the anthropologists, others are derived from such allied disciplines as paleontology, geology, zoology, and anatomy, to each of which the physical anthropologist is indebted for much of his own progress. No other science, however, attempts a true synthesis of human biology. This *is* physical anthropology.

Suggested Readings

Howells, W. W.
    1965. Some present aspects of physical anthropology. *Annals* of the American Academy of Political and Social Science, Vol. 357, Philadelphia.

Mead, Margaret
    1963. Anthropology and an education for the future. *The Teaching of Anthropology,* American Anthropological Assn. Memoir 94.

McKern, Thomas W. (ed.)
    1966. *Readings in Physical Anthropology.* Englewood Cliffs, N.J.: Prentice-Hall, Inc.

MAN IN NATURE

chapter
2

A gentleman named Webster, whose business it is to clarify things for us, has defined *taxonomy* as "1. the science of classification; laws and principles covering the classifying of objects. 2. classification especially of animals and plants into phyla, species, etc." This doesn't tell us much; chances are, we were able to relate taxonomy to classification before we made the long trek from desk to dictionary. We won't presume, of course, to attack the validity of Webster's statement. But we'd hoped to find embodied in that definition a sense of relevance—to man, to our world, to *us*. Most of us find little excitement in an endless lumping of technical names, related or not, but we can see enchantment in the discovery of the diversity of things. And so we view taxonomy as a tool of a larger science, *systematics*, which studies any existing relationships among the world's multitudinous varieties of life, past and present. In physical anthropology, we use taxonomy in order to view man as a part of the scheme of things. What kin does he have? From what ancestors does he derive? What is his place in nature?

Classification

The present system of classification stems from the work of *Carolus Linnaeus*, the famous eighteenth-century naturalist who believed that each species was separately created. He knew nothing of genetics. He attempted in no way to demonstrate kinship. He lived in a time prior to the acceptance of the evolutionary concept, when taxonomy served not to reflect phylogenetic relationships, but rather to demonstrate the orderliness of nature as it was divinely created.

Compared with the goals of present-day taxonomists, the efforts of Linnaeus were hardly ambitious; he sought only to name the living organisms and to group them within orderly categories. His organization, however, was sequential; that is, he included, within progressive stratified levels of classification, similar animals. The result, slightly modified, is an arrangement of classificatory levels in use even today. Each level includes all the units under it, much like the notes a student outlines from classroom lectures. An example of the current classification looks like this:

    Kingdom
    Subkingdom
    Phylum
    Subphylum
    Class
    Subclass
    Order
    Suborder
    Superfamily
    Family
    Genus
    Species

In this hierarchy, the progression from top to bottom is, in effect, from the general to the specific. For example, the kingdom *Animalia* includes any organism that is capable of movement, digestion, and respiration. Thus it is comprised of *all* animals, whatever their lesser or more restricted affiliations. Requirements for classification within the order *Primate,* on the other hand, can be met by fewer populations; the requirements are more *specific*. For inclusion, an organism must not only fulfill the requisites for inclusion within the higher levels (the kingdom *Animalia,* the subkingdom *Metazoa,* the phylum *Chordata,* the subphylum *Vertebrata*), but it must also exhibit the more specialized characteristics of the order *Primate*—that is, it must have a generalized structure, prehensile hands, a developed clavicle, nails, and two pectoral breasts. Later in this chapter, we will classify man throughout the taxonomic hierarchy in order to demonstrate the mechanics of classification. First, however, it is necessary to understand the criteria by which organisms are placed taxonomically, and the reasons behind those standards.

As we have noted, Linnaeus and his colleagues considered taxonomy an end in itself. Today classification is used to demonstrate evolutionary relationships. Indeed, the degree to which such relationships uncovered through other areas of scientific investigation correlate with established taxonomic classifications provides an evidence of its own for the evolutionary process.

Typological Approach

The early naturalists classified living organisms on the basis of their similarity to a model—the "ideal" or "typical" member of a population. Following establishment of this "ideal," animals were placed within (or excluded from) a particular category in accordance with their resemblance to that model.

Phylogenetic Approach

The fallacies in the historical system are evident: the typological approach failed to take into account the variability inherent in any population. No single representative can be termed "ideal." This is a vital awakening: too often a characteristic utilized for classificatory purposes varies within a population. We must search for stable traits or characteristics, held in common by all members of the population. When a population is genetically homogeneous (of like nature or composition) in possessing such traits, they may be applied in taxonomy. Thus, modern taxonomy has expanded upon the principles introduced during the eighteenth century. New terms, new criteria, new intermediate levels have been injected, all to demonstrate the degree to which organisms are similar or different. The goal of modern-day taxonomy is to refine the grouping system so that it will not only record groupings of forms, but also reflect the relationships among them.

This is not to imply that *morphology* (form and structure of organisms) fails to constitute a large and significant part of classification. Indeed, both historically and in the present, morphology is a basic tool. Its limitation in use lies in the recognition that variability does exist.

With respect to morphology, we apply a basic biological principle: *When anatomical structures look alike, they are related. When similarities are detailed, they constitute evidence of common ancestors.* We observe this principle almost daily, without conscious thought. We know, for example, that a dog is more closely related to a wolf than to a cow.

Similarities: Analogous and Homologous

Some similarities, however, are superficial. The classic example, perhaps overused but still graphic, concerns the wings of the bat and the bird. In both animals, the wing functions for flight. Functionally, the wings are similar. *Structurally,* they are not. Such superficial similarities are termed *analogous* and do not indicate relationship.

Consider next the foot of an ape and that of a man. The similarity between the two is structural. Functionally, they differ: in the ape, the foot is prehensile, while in man it is a highly specialized device for walking erect. Such similarities, despite differences in function, are termed *homologous;* these indicate evolutionary relationships.

At this point the student asks: How, then, may we explain the similarities found in the wings of the bird and bat? The answer lies in the process of *adaptation,* to be discussed in greater detail in later chapters. In simplest terms, however, we hypothesize that the roads to survival are apparently limited. Some animals, caught in new and changing environments, are forced to *adapt* to new conditions in order to survive. For example, the whale, who long ago exchanged terrestrial life for an aquatic environment, retained the basic structure of the land animal. Even though the whale is now restricted to the water and appears to the uninitiated much akin to a fish, he is classified as a mammal, for he possesses the characteristics of the class *Mammalia;* he is structurally mammalian. It is on such structural similarities that zoological relationships are based.

Yet the problems of classification are still more complex. After discounting analogous similarities, we must consider the fact that some similarities are more relevant than others. This is one of the difficulties encountered in classifying fossil forms, for more often than not, we unearth only partial remains of ancient skeletons. Further, we have found that a *total morphological pattern*—that is, a pattern of similarities throughout the body—is more revealing of kinship than a random collection of similarities. We search, then, for forms which have in common *complexes* of similarities.

Systematics, like physical anthropology, has come of age within the last century. It continues to grow, utilizing principles formulated in such allied sciences as serology, physiology, embryology, and psychology. And we become increasingly better equipped to classify man in time and space.

Now let's do so. Working with the simplified taxonomic hierarchy introduced earlier in the chapter, we will place man first within the largest groupings and work progressively toward the smallest group, which includes man as its sole representative.

The Classification of Man

KINGDOM

We have seen that the requisites for membership in the kingdom *Animalia* are the capacities for movement, digestion, and respiration. Forgetting for the moment that we know man not to be either vegetable or mineral, consider him as an organism:

he moves, he digests, he possesses a respiratory system. He is thus placed within the kingdom *Animalia*, and he shares such status with all other animals, from the insect to the extinct dinosaur.

SUBKINGDOM

There are two recognized subkingdoms into which *Animalia* is divided: *Protozoa* (single-celled organisms) and *Metazoa* (many-celled organisms). Man, because he is composed of many cells and reproduces himself through sexual reproduction, is classed as *Metazoa*.

PHYLUM

In determining the phylum to which man properly belongs, we consider two basic characteristics: (1) the dorsal central nervous system, and (2) axial symmetry. Man's nervous system is located dorsally, in the brain and along the spinal column. Further, he exhibits *axial symmetry;* that is, the right and left sides of his body are alike, as contrasted, for instance, with the starfish, which demonstrates *radial symmetry*. Man is thus placed within the phylum *Chordata*.

SUBPHYLUM

The criterion at the subphylum level is the presence of an internal segmented skeleton, which establishes man within the subphylum *Vertebrata*. An example of a nonvertebrate is the insect, which features an exoskeleton.

CLASS

It is at this level that man parts company with the fish, amphibians, reptiles, and birds. Man fulfills all the requirements for inclusion among the mammals:

>   1. He possesses mammary glands, through which his young are nourished;
>   2. He experiences *viviparous* birth; that is, his offspring are born alive, unlike those of the chicken, for example, whose

young are expelled encased in a shell within which they must further develop before hatching;

3. Man has warm blood, to aid in the maintenance of a stable body temperature;

4. Man possesses specialized dentition: that is, unlike the reptiles, whose teeth are similar to each other and whose dental function is restricted to grasping, mammals have dentition that is specialized to serve varying purposes—in man, the incisors act to cut and shear, the canines to tear, the molars to grind food;

5. Man has a differentiated vertebral column—its elements vary in shape and form according to location along the spine.

SUBCLASS

The class *Mammalia* is further divided into three parts on the basis of mode of reproduction. Among the *Prototheria,* of which the duck-billed platypus is a member, the young are encased in an eggshell, a rarity among mammals. The platypus is otherwise unquestionably mammalian. The *Metatheria* include the pouched animals, of which the opossum is a representative; these bear their offspring live but in an underdeveloped state, then protect them within the pouch until they can be safely subjected to the rigors of a natural environment. The *Eutheria,* of which man is a member, possess a *placenta,* that membrane composed of maternal and embryonic tissue which nourishes the human fetus during its nine-month development before birth.

ORDER

Man belongs to the order *Primates*. The criteria which place him within this grouping include (1) a generalized structure, (2) prehensile hands, (3) a developed clavicle, (4) nails on fingers and toes, and (5) two pectoral breasts. It is to this order that physical anthropologists direct the bulk of their attention, for the order *Primates* places man among his closest relatives: the tarsiers, lemurs, monkeys, and apes.

SUBORDER

The order *Primates* is further divided into suborders *Prosimii* and *Anthropoidea.*

The former grouping includes the lemurs, tarsiers, and tree-shrews. Among these, the tree-shrews are the most primitive. Indeed, some zoologists would deny them *Primates* status altogether. However, the fossil records, coupled with a total morphological pattern much like that of the lemurs, has led most experts to include them within the *Prosimii*. While the tree-shrews have claws rather than nails, all terminal digits show remarkable development toward mobility, particularly in the grasping function.

The lemurs, entirely arboreal and generally nocturnal, superficially resemble the monkeys but feature an elongated snout which suggests a more primitive status. Most possess both claw and nail. They date from early Tertiary deposits both in Europe and in North America.

The tarsiers, also small and arboreal, are represented by a single living genus. This animal is known chiefly for its distinctive modification of the hindlimbs, enabling it to leap with astounding agility through tree branches. Fossil tarsiers are found throughout the world, dating from early Tertiary deposits. Many experts believe that this group, or one closely related, may have provided the basis for the evolutionary development of the *Anthropoidea*.

The *Anthropoidea* include man, the apes, and the monkeys, on the basis of the following mutual characteristics: (1) eyes on a frontal plane, (2) stereoscopic vision (a close alignment of the eyes and a cross-network of nerve fibers project images upon the brain, which fuse to yield a depth perception not experienced by the remainder of the animal kingdom), and (3) a complete bony eye socket.

SUPERFAMILY

Among the *Anthropoidea* are the superfamilies *Hominoidea*, *Ceboidea*, and *Cercopithecoidea*. The *Ceboidea* include the New World monkeys (e.g., the spider monkey), while the *Cercopithecoidea* include the Old World monkeys (e.g., the baboon).

Man and the apes constitute the *Hominoidea*. The criteria for inclusion here are (1) the absence of external tails, (2) the absence of cheek pouches, (3) a dental formula of 2:1:2:3, and (4) a modified pelvis for upright posture.

The *dental formula* or *pattern* is derived from a count of the specialized teeth, beginning at the exact middle of both mandible (lower jaw) and maxilla (upper jaw). We count the number of each tooth form; that is, man's dental formula as noted above refers to the fact that he possesses, on each side of his jaws, both upper and lower, two incisor teeth, one canine, two premolars, and three molar teeth. Simple addition will reveal that if all teeth are present, they total thirty-two. We are considering, of course, *permanent* rather than *deciduous* (temporary) teeth.

FAMILY

At this level, man parts from the apes. As a member of the family *Hominidae*, he (1) exhibits a nasal bridge, (2) possesses a *philtrum* (the vertical fleshy groove extending from the base of the nose to the upper lip), (3) has a *lumbar curve* (the spinal structure which accompanies continual upright posture, (4) has a bony chin, and (5) exhibits true erect stance. The apes, which do not share these traits, are classified within the family *Pongidae*.

GENUS

For the *Pongidae*, genera include *Gorilla* (gorilla), *Pan* (chimpanzee), *Pongo* (orangutan), and *Hylobates* (gibbon). For *Hominidae*, the genus is *Homo;* it consists of man, wherever and whenever he appears.

SPECIES

At this classificatory level, the difficulties in nomenclature become most apparent, necessitating compromise and the temporary assignment of names in the interest of expediency. Such problems arise from the evolutionary process itself: progressive and continuous evolution results in an accumulation of changes, and no one has yet satisfactorily defined the point at which such changes justify an accompanying change in the name of an emerging species. However, most authorities now agree that a *species* can at least be defined as *a population which interbreeds to produce fertile offspring*. With this definition in mind, the genus *Homo* may be broken down into species.

During the past decades and continuing today, there has been heated dispute not only over the assignment of hominid status to the fossil forms which approximate man, but also over the specific differences which are apparent among them. This problem will be treated in later chapters. Certain of the ancient populations are now universally accepted, however (*e.g., Homo erectus,* the earliest undisputed true man; *Homo sapiens,* which appeared during the second interglacial period).

SUBSPECIES

The problems noted in the assignment of species designation are amplified and compounded at the subspecies level and will also be examined in later discussion. For the present, we can say that it is at this point that modern man is taxonomically separated from his fossil forms. *Homo sapiens sapiens,* or modern man, represents the subspecies unit. Another representative is *Homo sapiens neanderthalensis,* commonly termed Neanderthal Man. Experts are in general agreement that Neanderthal Man should occupy the same generic status as man. Most agree that, while no proof is available, Neanderthal Man would most likely fulfill the specific requirement for inclusion with modern man, but there are differences considered sufficient to warrant a subspecific separation.

The foregoing classification of man from kingdom to subspecies has served not only to demonstrate the mechanics of taxonomy, but also to point up some of the most vital questions in physical anthropology today. Perhaps the most complex is that of the evolutionary process itself, to be considered in theory and in fact over the following pages. Man's history on earth is a long one. It is not uncomplicated, nor is the history of its investigation. We will examine now the theories and contributions of the early anthropologists and their development of evolutionary thought.

Suggested Readings

Linnaeus, C.
   1758. *Systema Naturae,* 10th edition. Stockholm: Laurenti Salvii.

Muller, H. J.
   1957. Man's place in living nature, *Scientific Monthly,* Vol. 84, No. 3:245–54.

Simpson, G. G.
   1961. *Principles of Animal Taxonomy,* New York: Columbia University Press.

EVOLUTION —IN THEORY

chapter
3

Only a century and a half ago, man refused to delve into the mysteries surrounding his origins. Indeed, for the eighteenth-century man in the street, there *were* no mysteries. He had been taught—and he believed—that all living organisms, including man, had been divinely and separately created in their present form. Such a view precluded any developmental theory. Moreover, the doctrine of special creation was outside the realm of scientific verification, and any attempt to supplant the Biblical account of creation was viewed with alarm and hostility not only by the clergy but also by the leading scholars of the time.

As in any age, there were doubting voices raised. Some argued against special creation simply on the basis of the abundance of diverse life forms. Why, they wondered, should a Creator see fit to place separately upon the earth living forms in such infinite variety? A source of even greater discomfort to the advocates of special creation theory was the appearance, in ever increasing numbers, of human fossil remains. If man had no prehistory, how could these ancient forms be explained?

Catastrophism

One of the ablest proponents of the special creation theory was the well known and highly respected *Baron Georges Cuvier,* a French paleontologist. As such, he had viewed the graded changes of fossil remains within the geologic stratigraphy and was forced to admit that change through time was evident. This admission served, however, to enhance rather than to damage the view of special creation. Cuvier hypothesized that the world had been subjected to not one but a series of catastrophies, each one wiping out all existing populations. Further, he insisted, there had been a *succession* of special creations, one following each catastrophe. All living organisms dated from the last, that following the Biblical deluge; earlier forms, reflected in the fossil record, represented the products of previous creations. Man himself, according to Cuvier, did not exist prior to the Biblical creation. When, in 1823, Cuvier viewed a completely fossilized human skeleton unearthed from the banks of the Rhine River and associated with extinct animals, he rejected the find on the ground that man had no prehistory. The skeleton, he said, must be intrusive, accidentally mixed with animal remains from an earlier deposit.

In the same year, *Dean Buckland,* an English geologist and Catastrophist, recognized the need to reconcile fossil remains with the Mosaic chronology of Archbishop Ussher, who had dated the Biblical creation at 4004 B.C. Buckland himself helped to excavate Goat's Hole Cave in Paviland. When a human skeleton emerged in association with crude flint tools and extinct mammal remains, Buckland denied that association. The skeleton, he insisted, represented a later burial which had intruded into lower cave levels.

Developmental Theory

The Catastrophists continued to enjoy great popularity, and the view of the world as static and immutable retained its sanctity. It was in the face of such rigid intellectualism that *Charles Darwin* introduced a concept that even today provokes heated controversy.

Darwin was an unlikely candidate for the role of intellectual reformer. A shy, religious man of wealth and social prominence and lacking any appetite for fame, he hesitated more than twenty years before being persuaded by his friends and colleagues to publish *The Origin of Species.* This single volume, so cautiously authored and reluctantly printed, aroused a vigorous and undying interest in man's origins and past history, despite the fact that within its pages Darwin did not consider human populations.

Darwin's concept was not new; philosophers since the early Greeks had ventured repeatedly to suggest an evolutionary development for life forms. Darwin's expression of this same thinking, however, was heard. His essential achievement lay in his demonstration of a *mechanism* through which organic evolution, or change, appeared to be taking place. The mechanism: *natural selection.*

Darwin acted separately but not alone in formulating the principle at this time. *Alfred Wallace,* a biologist who had devoted extensive time to the study of fauna in the East Indies, had perceived a selective process that seemed to be operating among the animal populations he had observed. He wrote down his thoughts and sent them to Darwin.

In 1858, Darwin and Wallace presented parallel papers at the same scientific meeting, each describing the biological principle of natural selection. This was one of those amazing coincidences that occur in the history of scientific exploration. In a letter to *Charles Lyell,* the great pioneer in geology, and in remarks to his colleagues, Darwin told of his amazement at such a striking coincidence.

The thinking of both Darwin and Wallace had been shaped by the same man: *T. R. Malthus,* who had published, half a century before, his *Essay on the Principle of Population.* Malthus noted that human populations reproduce in geometric ratio, although space and available food supplies remain constant. In other words, the reproductive potential for man exceeds the natural resources necessary to support an ever increasing population. Malthus deduced that there must be some agent or agents (i.e., disease, drought, war, famine) acting to keep down surplus population.

Influenced by this view and by his years of personal observation, Darwin concluded that the various species of the world had not been separately created, as popularly assumed. Species were *mutable,* subject to change, and present-day groups must have evolved from earlier forms of life.

Darwin's Theory of Evolution

Darwin's theory, as presented in *The Origin of Species,* rested on three observed facts and two deductions based on these facts:

> *Fact 1:* There is a tendency for all organisms to increase in geometric ratio; that is, they reproduce more than their own number.
> *Fact 2:* In spite of this tendency to multiply, the numbers of a given species remain more or less constant.
> *Fact 3:* All living things vary. Offspring resemble but do not exactly duplicate their parents.
> *Deduction 1:* There is a struggle for existence, a universal struggle both between and within species for life.
> *Deduction 2:* Individuals with some advantage have the best chance of surviving and thus of reproducing their own kind.

Darwin saw that each species seemed to have a natural, balanced population density for any given environment, and yet more organisms are born in each generation than can possibly survive. The living must engage in a never-ending struggle for survival, a ceaseless battle for the available food supply and space. Only a fraction of the infants born live to become reproducing adults—the most fit fraction.

Which are the most fit? These need not always be the strongest nor the most ferocious. The most fit are rather those which, by virtue of some trait or traits, are best equipped to face the rigors of their environment. The lesser-suited individuals are eliminated; they die of disease or starvation, or become prey for the better-suited, in either case losing the opportunity to bear offspring similar to themselves. The most fit survive and multiply, passing on to their offspring the very traits which enabled them to survive to adulthood.

The passing on, through sexual reproduction, of superior traits or qualities represents change from generation to generation. To Darwin, *modification* or change of an organism usually meant greater adaptability. That is, new adaptations better equip the individual for survival in his own environment or enable him to exploit new environments, thus gaining additional resources. Any modification which increases the individual's chances for survival and reproduction would be preserved within the population; those changes that decrease survival chances would most likely be eliminated.

Such changes or adaptations have survival value in diverse ways. An example of moderate adaptation is found in the case of color differences. Consider, for instance, the defensive survival value of color in the chameleon, which, by blending into his environment, may escape the notice of would-be predators. The bears further illustrate this point: those found in snowy habitats are white, while woodland bears are brown or black. The degree or nature of adaptation, however, may also be extreme, as in the way that four-footed mammals gave rise through adaptive evolution to the bats and the whales, enabling these latter groups to reap the benefits of new environments and to escape the dangers of the old.

Any structure is somehow a result of variation, but Darwin was at a loss to explain variation itself.

Lamarck: Acquired Characteristics

One of those who attempted to explain variation was a French scholar with the formidable name of Jean Baptiste Pierre Antoine de Monet, Chevalier de Lamarck. *Lamarck* mistakenly assumed that characteristics which were acquired or lost during the lifetime of an individual were transmitted to the offspring. He believed that such transmission was accomplished through blood or some special body juice. Twentieth-century geneticists have thoroughly discredited Lamarkian theory, ignoring, unfortunately, the fact that Lamarck—despite his thinking with reference to acquired characteristics—did thoroughly understand the fact that evolution had taken place and further that he meticulously documented that occurrence. It was, however, without the benefit of advanced science that Lamarck was discredited during his lifetime.

Weissmann: Continuity of the Germ Plasm

In a successful attempt to demonstrate the absurdity of Lamarck's theories, the German zoologist *August Weissmann* collected a number of rats, removed their tails, and bred them. There were, of course, no tailless rats in the succeeding generations, proving—as Weissmann termed it—the *continuity of the germ plasm*. Despite his tongue-in-cheek experiments, he amply demonstrated that structural changes induced during the lifetime of the individual were not transmittable to the offspring. Thus attempts to improve upon nature in the adult do not result in permanent change.

It is interesting to note that twentieth-century neo-Lamarckists may enjoy the last laugh in this particular issue. Modern experiments with radiation have revealed that permanent change now may be induced in the adult cell and transmitted to succeeding generations.

Mendel: The Laws of Heredity

Although Darwin did not utilize them, the answers to his questions regarding variability were being formulated within a few years after the publication of *The Origin of Species*. *Gregor Mendel*, an Augustinian priest familiar with the mechanics of selective breeding, had experimented at length under strictly controlled conditions with plant hybridization. In 1865 he published his results, demonstrating a regular pattern of inheritance based on the transmission of "particles" from generation to generation.

In a typical experiment, Mendel selected plants which differed in a single characteristic, such as color. For example, he cross-fertilized yellow and green garden peas. In the resulting first hybrid generation, all the peas were yellow. Eager to explain the mysterious disappearance of the green, Mendel proceeded to self-fertilize this totally yellow generation. The resulting second hybrid generation consisted of both yellow peas and green peas, but in a 3:1 ratio.

On the basis of this and similar experiments, Mendel concluded that heredity is effected by the transmission of discrete particles. He had no way of knowing exactly what took place within the cell at the time of reproduction. His inferences, however, are sound. We know now that in sexual reproduction, *genes* (similar in principle to Mendel's "particles") provide the physical link between generations. They exist in great number and dictate the expression of individual traits in the offspring.

Reproduction, as understood by modern geneticists, will be treated in detail in a later chapter. For the present, it is necessary only to recognize the process by which offspring inherit their visible characteristics from their parents. In simple, generalized terms, the new individual develops from the *zygote* or fertilized egg, which is produced by the fusion of the sperm from the father and the ovum from the mother. Each contributing parent cell contains approximately 40,000 genes; thus it is possible for the fusion of only two minute cells to effect the transmission of thousands of physical characteristics.

Prior to reproduction, the parent sex cells (the sperm and the ovum or egg) undergo numerous changes, the most important of which is gene duplication. Keeping in mind that this operation takes place within the single cell, the student might wonder how, in so small a space, the duplication of thousands of genes might be effected in orderly fashion so that each daughter cell inherits one each of the parents' genes. The answer lies in the physical arrangement of the genes.

Through microscopic studies developed since Mendel's time, we have learned that genes do not exist as separate units, but are arranged in linear order along the length of the *chromosomes,* threadlike bodies housed within the cell nucleus. In man, there are forty-six chromosomes, each composed of thousands of genes. With such an arrangement, the cell can more effectively handle the duplication and segregation of great numbers of genetic units.

While Mendel lacked the knowledge of chromosomal arrangement, he correctly inferred that each parent contributes hereditary units to the offspring and that there exist alternate forms of genes. Modern geneticists know that each gene has a particular position on a particular chromosome. The position is termed the *locus* or location. Alternate gene forms are termed *alleles*. In oversimplified terms, in the yellow-green garden pea experiment noted previously, alleles for yellow and for green were present at the locus for color. In the first hybrid generation, yellow was *expressed,* or apparent physically. The alleles, or alternate forms, are segregated during the preparation of the reproductive cells. This is Mendel's *Law of Segregation*.

One gene form may be *dominant* over another. In our present example, yellow dominates over green; that is, when an individual garden pea plant inherits genes for both yellow and green (one from each parent) it is the yellow which is expressed in the *phenotype* (physical appearance) of the individual. The green, in this instance, is said to be *recessive;* it does not disappear but is carried in the *genotype* (the genetic make-up) of the individual. The recessive is seen in the phenotype only when recessive genes are inherited from both parents; in other words, the recessive is expressed only in the *absence* of the dominant allele.

This principle is illustrated diagrammatically in Figure 1. Assuming that we are working with two "pure" or homologous parents, one green and one yellow, we represent the parents by symbols indicating their genetic make-up: YY for homologous yellow, gg for homologous green. When these two individuals are cross-fertilized, the Hybrid 1 generation consists of individuals that are phenotypically yellow (because the gene for yellow is dominant over green) and genotypically heterozygous. In genetic shorthand, we have:

$$(YY)(gg) = Yg + Yg + Yg + Yg.$$

The potential for green, however, is not lost, as can be seen in the figure, for each individual has received contrasting genes from the parents. The potential for green, "masked" by the dominant yellow and therefore not visible, is retained in the genotype of each individual.

Assume now that we self-fertilize one member of the Hybrid 1 generation. The resulting Hybrid 2 generation is composed of the following individuals:

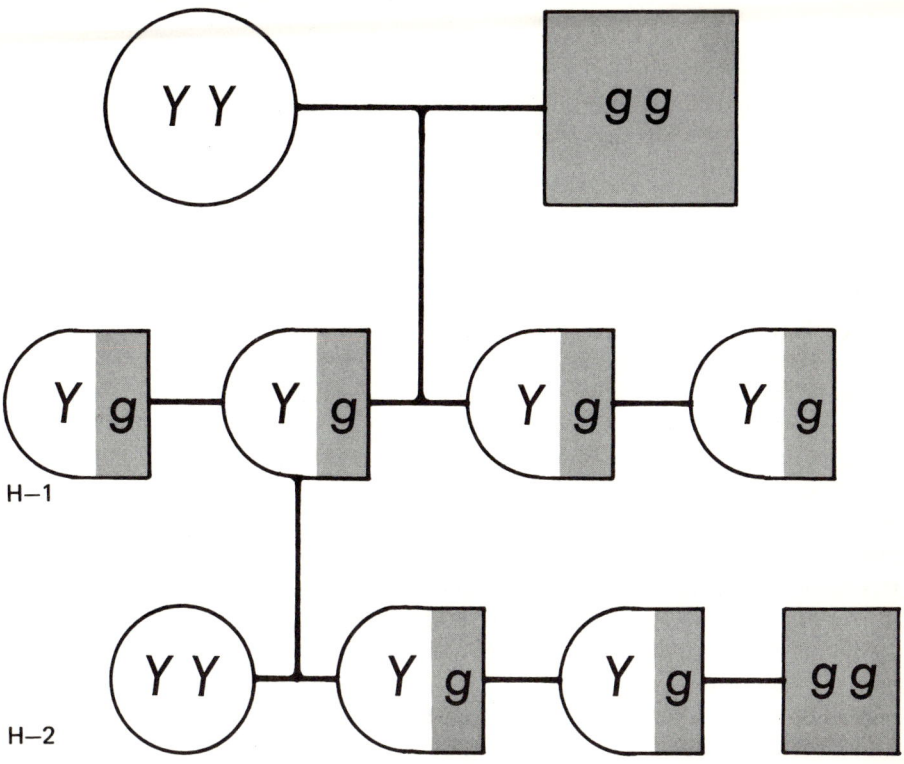

FIGURE 1 Schematic representation of Mendel's Law of Segregation.

1. *One YY individual:* YY is both phenotypically and genotypically yellow. It has inherited no genetic potential for green as it received, one from each parent, two genes for yellow;

2. *Two Yg individuals:* These are phenotypically yellow and therefore do not differ visibly from the YY individual discussed above. They are said to be *heterozygous;* they carry not only the dominant gene (Y) which is expressed, but also the recessive gene (g) which is masked;

3. *One gg individual:* The fourth member of Hybrid 2 generation is both phenotypically and genotypically green. It received no potential for yellow, having taken from each parent the gene for green. It is termed *homozygous recessive.* The recessive green is expressed only because the dominant yellow is absent.

One can quickly compute hereditary potential if the genetic content of parent individuals is known. For example, if we cross-fertilize Yg with Yg in the second hybrid generation, we have only to multiply:

$$(Yg)(Yg) = YY + Yg + Yg + gg.$$

Of course, a pea plant is more than color alone. It has form, shape, the capacity for blossoming, and so forth. Traits for these characters must be transmitted in the same way, simultaneously, as those for color. Mendel experimented in order to find out how differing pairs of potentialities are inherited. Selecting round yellow peas, he crossed these with wrinkled green peas. The first hybrid generation consisted of all round, yellow peas. This did not surprise him, for he knew yellow to dominate over green and round over wrinkled. Mendel continued, self-fertilizing this generation and producing peas of all combinations: round green, round yellow, wrinkled green, and wrinkled yellow. He concluded that the potential for shape was not connected with the potential for color. The characters were inherited independently of one another. This principle is known as Mendel's *Law of Independent Assortment*.

We know now that heredity is governed by many more complex principles than these two laws, and we will discuss later developments in Chapter 10. We should keep in mind for the present, however, that Mendel's experiments were sound; his discoveries ultimately formed the basis for modern genetic studies. Unfortunately, his work was never fully understood nor recognized during his lifetime, and it was not until the early part of the twentieth century that his investigations were rediscovered and utilized. Then and only then did genetics assume its present position of importance among the scientific disciplines that today form the basis for modern evolutionary theory.

Man and Evolution

So much for garden peas and tailless rats: how did man fit into this scheme of things? Darwin had not considered man in his *Origin of Species*. Within a few years, however, he became convinced that natural selection was not only responsible for the development of plants and other animals, but worked as well in the evolution of man. In 1871, Darwin published *The Descent of Man,* in which he presented his view that man had descended from an earlier primate form. He did not mean to imply, though many assumed it, that man evolved from a creature like the modern ape or monkey. He hypothesized rather that there had existed in the past an ancestor common to all primates, man included.

Darwin reached this conclusion primarily through a thorough study of anatomy. He had compared bodily structures, recognizing in the bones, muscles, nerves, and blood vessels striking similarities between man and other mammals. He also considered embryological studies, finding man's early development remarkably similar to that of other animals. His conclusion: that the mechanism of evolution must act upon man as upon other life forms. To Darwin, there was no other feasible explanation for the observed similarities.

One more point. Darwin never utilized the human fossil evidence that was beginning to accumulate in various parts of the world. Thus he ignored two of the most important areas of evidence in support of his theory—genetics and fossil man material. Yet these and other, later-developed studies have yielded what must be considered proof of the evolutionary process. Evolution in *theory* becomes evolution in *fact.*

Suggested Readings

Darlington, C. D.
   1959. The origins of Darwinism. *Scientific American,* Volume 200, No. 5:60–66.

Darwin, C.
   1859. *The Origin of Species.* London: Murray.

   1871. *The Descent of Man.* London: Murray.

Kettlewell, H. B. D.
   1959. Darwin's missing evidence. *Scientific American,* Volume 200, No. 3:48–53.

Mendel, G.
   1866. Experiments in plant hybridization. *Proceedings of the Natural History Society of Brunn* (English translation, Harvard University Press, 1948).

Weissmann, A.
   1892. *Essays upon Heredity.* Oxford: Oxford University Press.

EVOLUTION—IN FACT

chapter **4**

The process of evolution is often defined as *descent with modification*. *Descent*, of course, refers to heredity, the transmission of life from generation to generation. *Modification*, as defined by Darwin and as applied today, refers to adaptive variation, change through time in response to environmental pressures coupled with the universal will to survive. Put simply, evolution means that *all existing life forms, with their advanced and specialized organs, have grown out of preceding life forms through a natural process of modification*.

When Darwin formulated this single hypothesis, he offered the world a glimpse into its unknown past. The world, habitually skeptical, replied: *Show me*.

No single individual—not even one of such foresight and perception as Charles Darwin—could comply, nor can a single discipline today. The evidence for the evolutionary process is derived from many separate and diverse fields of inquiry: comparative anatomy, embryology, geography, serology, paleontology, genetics, and many more. In all cases, the evidence is based on inference. There is simply no way in which to prove events of the distant past. We can, however, rely upon the techniques and methodologies of numerous scientific fields in order to substantiate what we now know must have occurred. The following sciences are among those which have most graphically demonstrated and supported the facts of evolution.

Comparative Anatomy

Comparative anatomy deals with the investigation of morphological similarities between different classes of organisms, with emphasis on their structural relationships to each other and to man.

If we propose that all animals are related, then it follows logically that the most closely related forms are those which have descended more recently from a common ancestral stock. In short, degrees of kinship between forms are determined by assessment of anatomical similarities. We compare, then, the anatomy of living man with that of other animals, focusing our attention upon the primates. Just as kinship among living groups may be traced in this way, fossil forms approximating existing groups are termed kindred. We need note only the common morphological features which characterize a given group and search the fossil record for similar features. Further—keeping in mind that evolutionary trends are from the general to the specific—we can postulate the form of the ancestral stock from which a given existing group descended. It is possible, therefore, to hypothesize a "missing link," a probable ancient ancestor, without yet having discovered his actual fossil remains.

In assessing or proposing phylogenetic relationships, we bear in mind that noted similarities may or may not have evolutionary significance. Analogous similarities are discounted, for, as we have seen, it is the homologous resemblances which demonstrate degrees of kinship. Particular note is taken of the total morphological pattern. In many cases, numerous features together comprise the total form of a given anatomical structure, and often this combination of characters is under the control of a single gene, the alteration of which may affect the overall structure. We resist, then, the temptation to count individual, isolated characters.

The result is a taxonomic system based on proven relationships. In this system can be seen a history of life forms across the world.

Comparative anatomy seeks to explain such phenomena as *vestigial organs*. For example, the dissected body of a whale points up the presence of rudimentary hind limbs. The whale, totally adapted to an aquatic environment, has no use for legs. Their presence demonstrates an earlier land ancestry. So it is with the python, which has similar rudimentary legs.

Another classic example concerns the sightless fish that inhabit underground ponds or rivers and pools in dark caves. In these fish the eyes are structurally present but are depigmented and so do not function to provide sight. We must assume that the eyes did function in the ancestral stock but were reduced in later forms as a result of ceasing to play so important a role in survival as when they were initially developed.

In simple terms, vestigial organs are organs that have lost their original function; they either readapt to serve new functions (as in the whale, where the hind limbs now serve as fins to aid in aquatic locomotion) or become totally functionless (as in the case of the blind fish). This is adaptive modification in operation, changes in response to changing conditions.

Man himself presents myriad examples. He retains but (except for a few life-of-the-party types who have somehow retained the talent) cannot use muscles for moving his ears. He has muscles, too, for twitching his skin—much as a horse does in flicking flies away—but has lost the ability to use them. Tail bones provide another illustration: in man, they are present in rudimentary form, readapted to provide a floor for support of the pelvic organs. Another example is the appendix, serving no apparent function in man, though in various vegetarian groups it acts as a digestive aid. Experts in the field of comparative anatomy can find no reasonable explanation for these vestigial organs other than that they have been retained from a time in the past when an ancestral form did utilize them.

Embryology

Embryology is the *study of individual development in its earliest phases*. All complex animals develop from a single fertilized egg. By observing the growth and development of this simple cell, we can view what we have inferred from studies in comparative anatomy—that is, how complex forms arise from simple ones.

In 1828, *K. E. von Baer* published the results of his investigations on the development of animals. In his research, von Baer noted a remarkable similarity among embryonic vertebrates which, once developed to the adult stage, differed from one another. Later the noted biologist *Ernst Haeckel* modified this observation into a Biogenetic Law, often referred to as the *Theory of Recapitulation*. This theory states simply that *ontogeny recapitulates phylogeny*. In other words, the developmental stages of the embryonic individual repeat or review the evolutionary history of the group. As it is often said, man climbs his own family tree, repeating in the womb the evolutionary development of his species.

The proponents of this theory pointed to certain phases in human embryonic growth in an attempt to prove their thesis. For example, they cited the embryonic neck grooves, the tail, and the presence of the *lanugo* (a hairy covering over the human fetus at six to eight months' gestation) as representing evolutionary stages. But the recapitulationists go too far. It is true that the human embryo develops pouches in the throat region as well as corresponding furrows on the neck surface. These occupy the same position as gill pouches in fish, but the pouches in the human embryo do not open, nor do they assume the gill slit function or structure of an adult fish. Actually, they go on to develop other structures.

Other "evidence" for the recapitulation theory can be similarly explained away. In the light of modern embryological knowledge, we do not accept Haeckel's Law. Von Baer and Haeckel were not entirely wrong, however. The stages of development do appear to review the evolutionary phases of the group—but in the *embryonic* rather than the *adult* state.

Studies of ontogeny or embryonic development can be of use in exploring evolutionary history, but we must take care not to misinterpret our inferred evidence; we will continue to lack embryological data in the fossil record. We can, on the other hand, utilize comparative ontogeny in determining the degree of affinity between two groups of animals. The more similar the ontogeny, and the later in ontogeny the two animals diverge, the more closely related they are phylogenetically.

As an example of the work presently being undertaken in the application of embryonic studies to the question of human evolution, we turn to numerous dental studies. Experts have noted some striking parallels between human dental development and the postulated evolutionary process for human dentition.

Bertram S. Kraus, a noted physical anthropologist fully competent in the field of dentistry, found support for the principle of recapitulation in the molar development of man and of the rhesus monkey. Assuming that similar ontogeny points to genetic affinity, we can expect a late divergence in ontogenetic development among closely related animal groups. In fact, the later the divergence, the more closely related the groups. Comparing rhesus and human molars (see Figure 2), Kraus found that he could distinguish between the two at initial molar calcification. Human racial differences (distinction between Negroid, Caucasoid, and Mongoloid) could not be noted at this early stage, demonstrating that the divergence in ontogeny for the more closely related groups occurs later. Kraus rightfully argues for a reevaluation of modern recapitulation theory and provides strong evidence that embryology does play a vital role in supporting evolutionary theory.

Geography

The study of geography yields useful data not only on the world distribution of animal groups, but also on the effects of geographic environments upon the relationships between such groups.

Of primary relevance is the fact that isolation results in diversification within any group, an observation which helped shape Darwin's thinking on evolution. Instances of isolation are common: entire continents are separated from one another by vast expanses of water. Other geographic barriers are deserts, mountains, valleys, and even climatic differences. These barriers

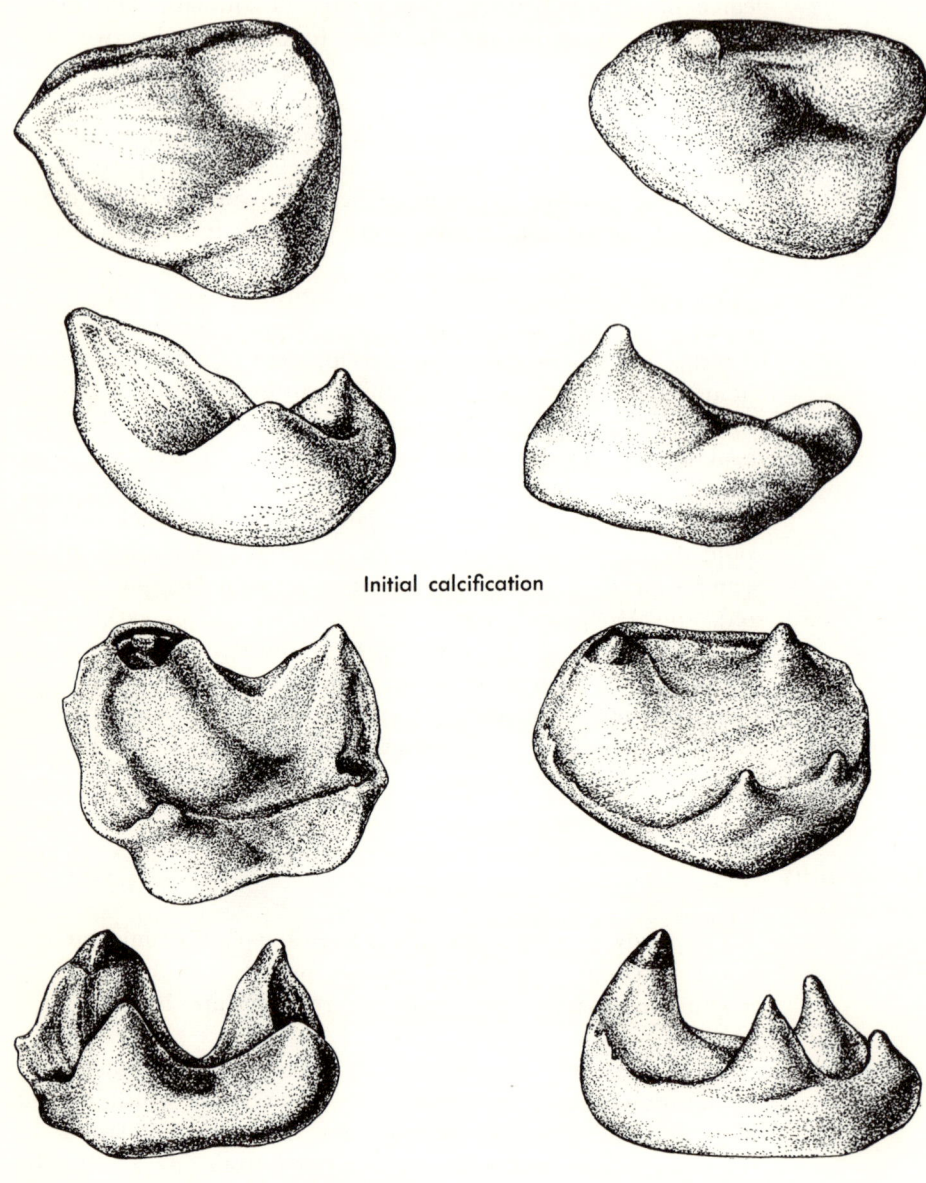

FIGURE 2 Comparison of molar development in rhesus and man. Redrawn from Figure 55 in *The Basis of Human Evolution* by Bertram S. Kraus (Harper & Row, 1964).

serve to separate land masses into distinct life zones, each with its typical flora and fauna. Free from the genetic influence of barred life forms, species within each zone develop on their own, and minor differences are apparent between species of even adjacent regions. This is termed *geographic determinism*. In order to demonstrate how geographic distribution relates to evolutionary theory, let's consider the implications of *Wallace's Line*, an imaginary boundary represented in the ocean by a set of deep troughs which separated the Asian and Australian continents. That life forms to each side of this line differ is obvious. But how can this faunal differentiation be explained?

During Eocene times—possibly earlier—water levels were down, and a land bridge connected southeast Asia with Australia. Animals roamed freely back and forth. Then the water levels rose, obliterating the land connection and keeping all land-dwelling animals from reaching New Guinea and Australia for millions of years.

Metatherian (marsupials, or pouched mammals) and prototherian (monotremes, or egg-laying mammals) forms were geographically isolated to the east and south of the line. They developed on their own without eutherian competition or interference. To the west and north, the eutheria (placental animals) reigned supreme. They were not introduced into Australia until late Pleistocene times. Here, then, is a case where a geographic barrier has permitted the persistence of an early evolutionary form; kangaroos and other marsupials remain abundant in Australia and New Guinea. They flourished only in the absence of the placental animals.

One further implication of Wallace's Line: since placental animals were barred from the east and south of the line, we can discount Australia entirely as the birthplace of man. There were no forms from which man could have evolved.

Serology

Serology, the *science of blood chemistry*, is probably, in potential, among the most valuable of the laboratory sciences in yielding supportive evidence for the process of evolution. Moreover, it provides a way to substantiate conclusions based on comparative anatomy.

Among the early serological studies from the physical anthropologist's viewpoint was the classic work by Nuttall on *Blood Immunity and Blood Relationships*.[1] Nuttall investigated the immunity reaction in many animal species, utilizing a precipitin test in which a member of one species is injected with the blood serum of a second species to the point of immunization. Then blood serum from both species is mixed in a test-tube environment. Nuttall found that a precipitate is formed when the two species are closely related, the degree of relationship correlating with the intensity of the precipitate reaction. Unrelated species produce no reaction upon mixture.

Such tests confirm morphological inferences with regard to the major taxonomic groups and provide a valuable tool for testing classification in that the tests are objective, can be expressed in quantitative terms, and—above all—are performed on a basic property of the organism: the biochemical make-up of blood protein.

At the order level, serological tests have clearly substantiated the close relationship of man to the nonhuman primates. Blood groups noted among the pongids are present also in man, as shown by Table I. It is interesting to note that Type O blood

TABLE I

Primate Blood Groups

	Blood Groups Observed			
Man	A	B	O	AB
Mountain Gorilla	A			
Lowland Gorilla		B		
Chimpanzee	A		O	
Orangutan	A	B		AB
Gibbon	A	B		AB

is rare among apes but common in man.

Blood similarity tests have been performed in an attempt to demonstrate the degree of kinship among primates. The results show that in total blood chemistry, the chimpanzee is most like

[1] Nuttall, G. H. F. *Blood Immunity and Blood Relationships* (Cambridge: Cambridge University Press, 1904).

man; the orangutan, gorilla, baboon, and New World monkeys follow in that order.

Numerous attempts have also been made to cross-match and transfuse blood between chimp and man. This has been successfully accomplished—that is, human blood has been given to chimpanzees with good results.

Paleontology

In paleontology—the *science of previous life forms as represented by fossil animals and plants*—the physical anthropologist has a means by which to demonstrate the phylogenetic relationships he has postulated. Based firmly on the time-tested principles of geology, the paleontological record exhibits a succession of transitional stages in the development of animal groups through time. We have in this record a temporal sequence of life: how the early forms looked, what changes occurred in their morphology, how they differentiated in time and in space.

However, caution is essential in applying the paleontological evidence. There are frustrating gaps in the fossil record. In many regions, climatic conditions are unfavorable for the preservation of remains through fossilization. Unfortunately, this is particularly true for the primates, whose crucial evolution apparently occurred in tropical or subtropical areas. Further, it is often only by accident that remains are found; the hope of unearthing a given "missing link" is slim. Moreover, when even both preservation and excavation occur, many remains are discovered in a fragmentary condition; often, they are represented only by bones and teeth and the meager inferences which may be made from these about the soft parts of the body. Problems of dating and interpretation must be considered. And a totally complete sequence is never preserved nor found.

Despite these serious limitations, paleontology can and does provide objective evidence for evolutionary trends. As the accumulation of finds continues, the fossil record becomes increasingly more reliable. The importance of this record cannot be too strongly emphasized. In later chapters, we will discuss the significant fossil discoveries and the inferences made from these remains.

Genetics

Genetics—the *science of organic inheritance*—assumes ever-increasing importance in supporting evolutionary theory. Until the basic structural phenomena which produce organic change are known, the formation, development, and differentiation of faunal groups can never be fully understood. Genetics is the key to a clear understanding of both the past and the future—the basic mechanisms of inheritance, how one generation passes on its physical characteristics to the next, and how changes do take place.

Within the next pages, we will examine some of this evidence, beginning with the geologic time zones and the fossil history of the lower primates.

Suggested Readings

Darlington, P. J.
    1957. *Zoogeography: the geographical distribution of animals.* New York: John Wiley and Sons.

Kraus, Bertram S.
    1964. *The Basis of Human Evolution.* New York: Harper & Row.

Needham, J.
    1931. *Chemical Embryology.* Cambridge: Cambridge University Press.

GEOLOGIC TIME

chapter
5

There is little argument today that man shares with other primates a close biological relationship, arising from a process of gradual diversification through time from an early mutual ancestor. As we have seen in preceding chapters, however, when Darwin and others first advanced this hypothesis, inferences were drawn almost solely from observation of morphological similarities between man and the anthropoid apes. No fossil record existed, and what little direct evidence was available was held largely in dispute by the authorities.

We have seen that morphological affinities between two taxonomic groups do play an important role in linking related forms. However, in order to demonstrate that evolution has indeed occurred, it is necessary to have direct evidence in the form of a temporal sequence, showing intermediate groups leading ultimately to living species. Scientific vindication of evolutionary theory as fact, then, rested upon the future discovery of ancient remains.

Happily, evidence began to appear. Nineteenth-century industrialization demanded new construction—of roads, buildings, mines, and quarries, and such construction led to the accidental discovery of fossil remains. The problem took on new dimension: it no longer lay primarily in the acquisition and stockpiling of evidence, but rather in the correct assessment of such material as it appeared.

When direct evidence for the course of human evolution comes to light—usually in the form of ancient bones or teeth—it is significant only if we are able to determine its age. The methods by which human material is dated are identical with those procedures utilized by geologists in dating rocks. For example, early geologists noted that sedimentary rocks, through the force of gravity, form beds laid down on land or in water. These beds may be composed of organic material, precipitates from water (e.g., salt), or fragmented rock transported by air or water from another locale. Whatever their origin, these beds collectively exist in layers called *strata* (singular, *stratum*); the study of strata is termed *stratigraphy,* and provides our key to geologic time.

Law of Superposition

Perhaps the single most important principle gleaned from the science of geology and set to use in anthropology in attempting to date human remains is the *Law of Superposition*. This principle refers to the fact that, in undisturbed layers, time is indicated by the sequence of deposition. In other words, *any stratum is older than the stratum above it, and younger than the one below.* Thus it is possible to place remains stratigraphically in temporal sequence in order to determine their age (see Figure 3).

Trained geologists are able to reconstruct past events in the earth's history. In this way, the Law of Superposition may be applied even though the sedimentary rocks have been disturbed. Working diagrammatically, the geologist notes the present terrain features, then proceeds mentally to "remove" the effects of each disturbing event. For example, if a study of surface conditions reveals evidence of heavy erosion, the geologist "removes" such effects, reconstructing conditions as they existed before erosion occurred. The same procedure is applied to stratigraphic disturbances arising from faulting, volcanic action, sliding, or

FIGURE 3 Schematic representation of the *Law of Superposition*. In the diagram, (1) represents the uppermost layer of earth. Found on the surface were remains of modern rodent (A); (2) represents the first layer below surface layer, within which was found (B), a stone dart point. Layer (3) yielded no remains. At the uppermost part of layer (4) human skeletal remains (C) were unearthed. Bones of an extinct variety of ground sloth (D) were found in layer (5). Layers (6) and (7) yielded no artifacts or skeletal remains. Below (7) is bedrock. In this hypothetical excavation, since stratigraphy is undisturbed, the *Law of Superposition* may be applied: we conclude that (D) is older than (C), which is older than (B). (A), the surface find, is the most recently deposited specimen.

other natural phenomena, and results in a diagrammatic reconstruction of the terrain and subsurface conditions as they were at points distant in time.

Fossils and Life History

In studying the earth's strata, geologists often recover *fossils,* the remains or evidence of ancient organisms. A dead animal may become fossilized in numerous ways, particularly if it possesses hard parts and is buried immediately. Most fossils are formed in shallow water, where sediment is constantly and rapidly deposited; hence the abundance of marine fossils. Land plants and animals may also become preserved, though in lesser numbers since conditions on land do not favor accidental preservation. Fossilization may be partial or complete: if the organic remains dissolve, molds or casts may be left in the sediment which accurately reflect the superficial characteristics of the dead animal. Under certain conditions, mineral matter may *replace* organic material (*petrifaction*) so that the organism may be duplicated, in whole or in part. Often only trails and tracks are found, but these too provide clues to the existence on earth of organisms never seen in life by man.

Faunal Succession

Eventually geologists noted a relationship between fossils and the arrangement of strata, and additional study made possible the correlation of deposits in widespread parts of the world. Even more important, at least in the study of evolution, was the discovery that when fossil remains are arranged in temporal sequence, there becomes apparent a trend toward specialization and increased efficiency of form; the older specimens are collectively less complex and less specialized than those of recent time, thus substantiating the theory of *progressive* evolution.

It is now evident that groups of fossils, both floral and faunal, succeed each other in an order progression, and each period of time can thus be determined, to a large extent, by the fossils characteristic of it.

Geologic Time Scale

On this basis, geologists have reconstructed a time sequence for the history of life on earth. This time scale is divided into large units termed *eras;* these are subdivided into *periods,* which are in turn reduced to *epochs.* Life history is summarized in Table II, which correlates time periods with those evolutionary advances characteristic to each.

Examination of the table will reveal the evolutionary tendency toward greater complexity and specialization. During the Archeozoic, living forms were unicellular; that is, all life processes were carried on, quite simply, within the individual cell. During Proterozoic times, single-celled individuals grouped together in colonies, as evidenced by the coral reefs, and many other organisms began to utilize calcium for building protective shells about their bodies. While most life forms at this time were immobile and thus dependent for food supplies on their abilities to sift surrounding mud or sea water, a few varieties (*e.g.,* the *trilobites*) were able to move about on their own power. Methods of locomotion during the early Paleozoic were poorly developed; even limited movement, however, made available greater food supplies and greater opportunities for eluding predators.

More complex organisms appeared, among them the first jawless fish; though these were doomed to extinction within their own era, they left descendants better equipped for survival. From them arose, toward the middle of the Paleozoic, the *Choanichthyes,* fishes able to take in air through their nostrils as well as their mouths. From the earlier lungfish also evolved the lobe-finned fish, the *Crossopterygians,* which are intermediate between primitive fish and later land-dwelling vertebrates.

It was in Devonian times that certain varieties of the lobe-finned fish made their successful transition from water to land. This accomplishment involves structural adaptation: a conversion of the fin to a walking limb, increased lung efficiency, and

TABLE II

Geologic Record

Era	Period	Epoch	Time (Years before present)		Life Forms
CENOZOIC	Quarternary				
		Recent	0–	8,000	
		Pleistocene	8,000–	2,000,000	Man
	Tertiary				
		Pliocene	2,000,000–	12,000,000	Proto-hominids
		Miocene	12,000,000–	28,000,000	Pongid radiation
		Oligocene	28,000,000–	40,000,000	Pongids
		Eocene	40,000,000–	60,000,000	Cercopithecoids
		Paleocene	60,000,000–	70,000,000	Prosimians
MESOZOIC	Cretaceous		70,000,000	130,000,000	Dinosaur peak; Toothed birds; Pouched, placental mammals
	Jurassic		130,000,000–	170,000,000	Reptiles; pre-marsupial mammals; True birds
	Triassic		170,000,000–	190,000,000	Reptiles, archaic mammals
PALEOZOIC	Permian		190,000,000–	550,000,000	Decline of amphibians
	Carboniferous				Amphibians; first reptiles
	Devonian				Peak of fishes; first amphibians, winged insects
	Silurian				Armored shark; first land forms (scorpions)
	Ordovician				Corals First jawless fish
	Cambrian				Marine invertebrates
PROTEROZOIC			550,000,000–	900,000,000	Primitive marine invertebrates
ARCHEOZOIC			900,000,000–	1,500,000,000	Unicellular life

50

more complex circulatory and excretory systems. The backbone is strengthened, for the weight of the animal must now be supported against the pull of gravity. The advantages of land-life, for those organisms able to accomplish the transition, were multiple and obvious: freedom from the increased competition in the seas, new and abundant food sources, and greater protection from predators.

At some time during the Carboniferous (Mississippian-Pennsylvanian periods) of the late Paleozoic, the first reptiles arose from existing amphibians. The major evolutionary advance accompanying such an improvement involves the reptilian ability to produce an egg which may be laid (and later hatched) on land. The young, encased in shell with food, water, and oxygen supplies assured, enjoy increased security against predators. This advantage is evidenced by heavy population increases, favoring the diversification which was to become characteristic of life in the Mesozoic.

Life flourished as the Mesozoic era dawned. The climate, moist and warm, encouraged dense vegetative growth and the creation of great swamps. In this atmosphere, reptilian life peaked; the fossil record teems with strange and exotic forms, many of gigantic proportions and many highly specialized for life in the air, in water, and on land. Birds appeared, as did the first small mammals, both dominated in number and variety by the great dinosaurs. Toward the end of the Mesozoic, however, there occurred a gradual lowering of the earth's temperatures, resulting in the disappearance of the immense swamps and the extinction of the dinosaurs. Reptilian life was decimated: left behind at the turn of the era were crocodiles, birds, and primitive mammals.

During Tertiary times, conditions were ideal for mammalian radiation. Food supplies were abundant, and, with the demise of the great reptilian forms, space and opportunity for survival were unlimited. Mammalian advantages are obvious; while mammals produce offspring in fewer numbers than do reptiles, the capacity for *viviparous* (live) birth, coupled with the extended period of parental association and protection, assured survival in higher numbers. Other advantages include warm blood, efficient reproductive systems, sturdy skeletons, milk glands, and —perhaps most important—the gradual enlargement of the mammalian brain.

The first prosimians appeared, followed by the cercopithecoids and pongids. During Miocene times, mammalian dominance peaked, and the pongid radiation became world-wide. The Pliocene carried with it the first proto-hominids, and the Pleistocene belonged to man.

We will consider the fossil primates in detail in later chapters. Dating techniques, however, deserve immediate attention, for in more recent times a difference of a few thousand years (hardly a second in time during the Paleozoic) is of great significance in determining the history of man.

Geochronology

In the preceding section, we have briefly summarized a few major evolutionary trends, viewing the history of life on earth as a progression from relative simplicity toward greater complexity and increased efficiency. How are we able to formulate such an evolutionary scheme? How do we know, for example, that the reptilian form arose from primitive amphibians or that *Homo sapiens* appeared first in the Pleistocene?

In order to follow the history of man, or that of any other living group, it is imperative that we be able to place, *in temporal sequence,* the events which comprise evolutionary development. In order to accomplish this, it is necessary first to assign dates for such events. Geochronology—the *science of dating*—involves the chronological arrangement of fossil evidence, and employs both relative and absolute techniques in an attempt to discover and trace evolutionary relationships.

Relative dating involves the placement of a specimen (event) with reference to other evidence within the temporal sequence. Numerous techniques have been developed, the most common of which are discussed below:

1. *Typological dating:* This early technique considers the form or structure of the specimen with reference to the evolutionary trend toward greater complexity. In other words, the simpler forms are the most ancient, while complexity denotes more recent age. This is a comparative device, largely subjective; its usefulness has been replaced by more scientific approaches to the problem.

2. *Geological stratigraphy:* Discussed in fuller detail earlier in this chapter, this technique utilizes the Law of Superposition

and assigns a geologic age for the specimen in question on the basis of the age of the deposit within which it is buried. The evidence, however, is subject to further tests. Is the bone contemporaneous with the stratum in which it is found, or does it derive from older (or younger) deposits, having been accidentally deposited in alien layers? For example, the *Galley Hill* skeleton, discovered in 1888, was once credited with great age on the basis of its burial medium. In 1948, however, Oakley and Montagu (Oakley, 1966) demonstrated, after testing the chemical composition of the bone in comparison with that of other bones characteristic of the deposit, that *Galley Hill* represents an intrusive burial. In actuality, this evidence dates from no earlier than post-Pleistocene times.

3. *Pollen analysis:* One of the most significant methods in geochronology, this test involves the extraction of pollen samples from the site under examination. A microscopic study of ancient pollen yields information regarding the climate of the region at points distant in time.

4. *Fluorine analysis:* A trace-element test, fluorine analysis is often performed on bone in an attempt to determine its relative age. The technique depends upon the proven premise that buried bone changes in chemical composition through time. Bone takes from its burial medium (the soil) minute quantities of fluorine. Stated simply, the older the bone, the more fluorine it contains, or the higher the fluorine content. This is the test which revealed the true age of the *Galley Hill* remains mentioned above. Fluorine analysis is primarily valuable in isolating remains which are *intrusive,* bones which are deposited through natural causes with the burial under examination.

Absolute dating, as opposed to the relative methods, measures age in terms of years. Representative techniques are outlined below:

1. *Dendrochronology:* Tree-ring dating provides excellent seasonal records. The width and spacing of the rings are fashioned by the effects of temperature, light, and moisture, all of which vary seasonally. The study of tree rings has yielded valuable information regarding the age of individual archeological sites, especially in arid regions where wood is most easily preserved. A continuous sequence has been devised which dates back some five hundred years; even longer chronologies are available for certain regions, including the sequoia forests of California.

2. *Varve analysis:* Like dendrochronology, varve analysis reflects seasonal variations, but this test also reveals a sedimentary record illustrating climatic conditions. A varve consists of a two-part *core*, taken from sedimentary rock, which shows melting and freezing conditions at times past. During warm periods, melted water from glaciers deposits sediment in lake bottoms, later to be seen in the wide band in the core. During periods of freezing, water ceases to flow and there is little or no sedimentation; therefore, winter seasons are represented in the core as narrow bands. The technique is valid, on the basis of the existing varve record, for almost seven thousand years into the past.

3. *Archeomagnetism:* This recently developed dating technique depends upon the peculiarities of the earth's magnetic forces to yield dates from fired clay with an accuracy of within fifty years.

Contrary to popular thinking, the geomagnetic north pole—which guides compass points—is not stable, but drifts constantly, shifting as much as six hundred miles every hundred years. This phenomenon permits dating of hearth clay excavated from archeological sites. By calculating the path of the earth's magnetic field at the time the clay sample was fired, and comparing the present magnetic direction, such experts as *Dr. Robert L. DuBois,* a geologist at the University of Arizona, can determine an age for that sample.

This technique is best utilized to complement dates obtained by methods such as the Carbon-14 technique.

4. *Carbon-14:* The Carbon-14 method has been perhaps the most impressive development in geochronology in recent years. Carbon-14, a radioactive isotope, is continually created in the atmosphere and enters into organic compounds of all types, to be assimilated by living organisms. As long as life continues, new Carbon-14 is added at a rate in balance with that of disintegration. With the death of the organism, however, no new radiocarbon is taken on, and the Carbon-14 content falls at an orderly rate. At approximately 5760 years after the time of death (termed the *half-life*), the rate of disintegration falls from the original 15.6 to a new rate of 7.8. Thereafter, the rate of disintegration is reduced by one-half each 5760 years. By measuring the amount of carbon remaining in the sample, and knowing

the rate of disintegration, one can calculate a date which represents the time at which the organism ceased to live.

Any organic material (bone, charcoal, seeds, shell, wood, etc.) may be subjected to the Carbon-14 test. Because many ancient artifacts are composed of organic materials, anthropologists have been quick to reap the benefits of this technique. The method is now valid only within the Cenozoic, however; after about seventy thousand years, the amount of Carbon-14 remaining in the sample is too small to be measured with existing procedures.

5. *Potassium-argon:* Another trace-element test, this method has also made valuable contributions to the science of dating. K-40, a radioactive isotope of potassium, has a half-life of 1,350,000,000 years; it diminishes at a known rate of disintegration into either Calcium-40 or Argon-40, which is a gas. Measurements and calculations are made on the basis of the rate of disintegration and the amount of trace element remaining, as in the Carbon-14 test.

Also valuable in determining geologic age are radioactive transformations from uranium to lead, thorium to lead, and rubidium to strontium.

Limitations of Radioactive-dating Methods

While the theories behind the use of trace elements in age determination are relatively simple, results of application have failed to yield constant figures. Difficulties arise from unresolved questions regarding the original state of the earth and its chemical constituents, and from the strictly mechanical uncertainties in the use of infinitely small amounts of material. The chief limitations arise from the fact that dates derived from small samples or areas cannot be meaningfully related to their surroundings.

The Carbon-14 test has been criticized on the basis of the many inconsistent or obviously incorrect dates derived. Discrepancies may stem from addition or subtraction of carbon following the time of burial (*contamination*). We must consider too the possibility that the original hypothesis underlying the method is invalid; it has been suggested that the rate of Carbon-14 production has not been constant over the last tens of thousands of years.

The potassium-argon method has yielded the most consistent results to date, and this technique is being applied presently with a high rate of reliability.

Whatever the limitations, radioactive-dating techniques will continue to be improved. With advances continually being made in atomic research, we may expect that dating technology will be applied in the future with increasing consistency and reliability, and that reasonable explanations will be found for most of the discrepancies now evident.

Suggested Readings

Deevey, Edward S., Jr.
   1952. Radiocarbon dating. *Scientific American,* Volume 186, No. 2:24–28.

Huxley, J. S.
   1953. *Evolution in Action.* New York: Harper & Row, Inc.

Oakley, Kenneth P.
   1966. *Frameworks for Dating Fossil Man* (2d ed.). Chicago: Aldine Publishing Company.

Romer, A. S.
   1959. *The Vertebrate Story.* Chicago: Chicago University Press.

Runcorn, S. K.
   1966. Corals as paleontological clocks. *Scientific American,* Volume 215, No. 4:26–33.

Simpson, G. G.
   1953. *The Major Features of Evolution.* New York: Columbia University Press.

Young, J. Z.
   1950. *The Life of Vertebrates.* Oxford: Clarendon Press.

THE FOSSIL PRIMATES

chapter
6

In the preceding chapters, we have defined the evolutionary process and viewed it as a dynamic force, shaping form through time. From this thought, it is but a short mental leap to the conclusion that evolution has sped along in orderly manner in a predetermined course, to culminate ultimately in modern man. Such an assumption is doubly faulty.

Orthogenesis

Orthogenesis—the concept that evolution is guided by unknown forces along a predestined direction—rears its head whenever the fossil record is accorded only cursory attention. The advocate of this view sees in paleontological history a succession of transitional forms, linked by their progressive development toward the present. He fails to note those short-lived forms which, doomed to extinction, leave no descendants to represent their existence in later periods. It is only by ignoring the evidence of the unsuccessful lines and concentrating solely upon surviving lineages that we see the illusion of orthogenesis. There is no evidence to support a view of predestination. Indeed, the principles of natural selection preclude such a concept as applied to organic evolution.

It is equally misleading to consider *Homo sapiens* the culmination of evolutionary progress. To be sure, modern man represents the most successful of all species. He is the most recent product of evolution, the most durable, the most intelligent. He alone in the animal kingdom possesses the means to manipulate his own environment and, to a certain extent, his own destiny. But to consider man the *final* product of evolution is to deny that he is subject to the action of natural law. Evolution does not stop with man.

Of course, it is with man that we are most directly concerned. We want to know ourselves, our origins, and our history. To do so, we focus not on man alone, but on the entire order from which man springs, to view *Homo sapiens* against the larger background of primate development.

Developmental Trends Among the Primates

While we can discount the mysterious forces of predestination, we do note certain developmental trends. These emerge and are shaped by the trial-and-error of evolutionary progress. They reflect adaptations among a group of animals to a common environment and way of life. For the primates, such trends are prompted by modifications in response to arboreal life.

Life in the trees is quite a different proposition from life on the ground. New abilities rate high in survival value, while old ones are discarded as their importance diminishes. As the primates took to the trees, numerous anatomical changes occurred. While it is difficult to sort these out and place them in exact chronological order, we can observe certain closely related modifications which effectively paved the way toward primate survival.

In tracing such developmental trends, we draw from data supplied by the fields of paleontology and comparative anatomy. Dentition, for example, is accorded close attention; it is impossible to emphasize too strongly the importance of the dental record. The teeth, composed of dentine and enamel, comprise the most durable portion of the skeleton. For this reason, of all bodily parts, the teeth are most often preserved to present to us the existence of an ancient form. It is possible, when only the teeth are found, to represent a fossil population and to hypothesize kinship on this evidence alone. In many cases, such hypothesized relationships have been confirmed later, when more comprehensive evidence came to light. Moreover, the teeth are morphologically stable. An undeveloped tooth germ, transplanted to tissue culture and isolated from its natural environment, will develop normally to its characteristic cusp pattern, as demonstrated as early as 1938 by S. Glasstone.[1]

Heterodonty—the regional differentiation of tooth form to serve diverse purposes—is a major mammalian characteristic, which appeared early in the developmental history of the mammals. The Eutherians, arising from a mammalian order known as *Pantotheria*, inherited the heterodont condition in a high degree of efficiency. The Pantothere dentition was not only of great functional advantage at the time, but it featured a molar cusp pattern easily adaptable to varied modifications. It is this adaptability that permitted widespread radiation of the early Eutherians, favored as they were with dentition capable of dealing with the most diverse environments.

We know from the fossil record that the early Eutherian dental formula was 3:1:4:3—that is, a hypothetical primate ancestor featured on each side of both jaws three incisor teeth, one canine, four premolars, and three molar teeth. In both the premolars and the molars there was present a *cingulum*, an enamel ridge of evolutionary significance. It is the cingulum which, by forming a foundation for additional cusps, permits increased crown complexity.

From this early model, from which the early primates evolved, can be traced certain characteristic deviations or trends for the Primate order as a whole:

1. *Reduction in the number of incisor teeth:* In almost every known member of the Primate order, there are two rather than three incisors. The only living exception is the tree-shrew, which features in its lower jaw the full primitive complement, as do a few fossil tarsiers.

[1] Glasstone, S. A comparative study of the development *in vivo* and *in vitro* of rat and rabbit molars. *Proceedings of Royal Society* B, 126:315, 1938.

2. *Hypertrophy of the canine:* In most primates, the canine has become elongated and strengthened into a sharp defense weapon, as in the larger monkeys. In *Homo sapiens* and certain other modern forms, there has occurred a secondary reduction in size; that is, the canine, following hypertrophy, has reduced again. In these cases, the canine is hardly distinguishable from the incisor series.

3. *Reduction in number of premolar teeth:* With the exception of the prosimians and ceboids, modern primates possess only two premolars, a halving of the primitive number. In the surviving premolars is seen a strong tendency toward *molarization;* that is, additional cusps grow up from the cingulum, so that the premolars look and function much like the neighboring molar teeth. In the lower primates, molarization is extreme; in man and the pongids, cusp addition is limited to a single second cusp, located medially to the original one.

4. *Increased crown complexity in molar teeth:* The three-cusped (tritubercular) form has given way in time to a quadritubercular form by the addition of a fourth cusp.

The preceding trends in dental evolution were set in motion with the early development of the primate skull, in turn a response to the expansion and gradual reorganization of the internal brain. These trends, and others characteristic of the primate order, are traced back to an early adaptation to arboreal life. For example, limb development functionally advantageous to climbing and grasping occurs early in primate history. The grasping function has particular significance: the upper limbs, once freed by erect posture, can be used for hand-feeding, a service heretofore performed by the teeth. Assuming this evolutionary event, it requires no great mental labor to explain the reduction in size and/or number of individual teeth.

Modifications in the brain and the skull are similarly explained. First and most distinctive is the expansion of brain size in proportion to total body weight, a tendency noted first in the early mammals and reaching a peak of refinement in the primate brain. Among the primates, this expansion is accompanied by an elaboration of the convolutions on the surface of the cerebral cortex. Quite apart from this elaboration, but equally relevant, is the modification of the internal organization of the brain itself.

Among mammals the cerebral cortex is regionally differentiated into sensory areas. In the primitive brain, these areas are vaguely differentiated, but it is characteristic of the primate brain that such areas can be more easily determined in disposition and extent. Here the impact of new values on morphology is obvious: in the early terrestrial mammal, a large proportion of the brain is devoted to the olfactory function, for on land the sense of smell is crucial. In arboreal life, smell has reduced value. Infinitely more important to survival is sight. Accordingly, the visual area of the primate brain is expanded, while the olfactory region is greatly diminished.

Such neural modifications are reflected in the skull itself. The expansion of brain size is necessarily accompanied by a tendency toward great cranial capacity. Associated with this increased size is a rounded surface for the effective attachment of masticatory muscles, eliminating the need for the bony crests noted elsewhere in the animal kingdom.

Jaws are reduced in response to the newly efficient employment of the forelimbs. The snout is reduced, due in part to the decreased jaw size but also influenced by the reduced olfactory function and the enhanced need for visual acuity. With decreased snout, the eyes can lie close together, facing forward. They are protected by enlarged orbital cavities and surrounded by a complete bony eye socket.

Brachiation—movement through the trees by hanging and swinging by the forelimbs—forces vertical posture, and this upright stance is reflected not only in the post-cranial skeleton but also in the skull itself. The *foramen magnum* (that cranial opening through which the spinal cord emerges), which is placed at the back of the skull in *pronograde* (horizontal) animals, changes its position in the *orthograde* (vertical) primate, lying in a more forward position at the skull base. This development changes the axis of the skull, so that the face, greatly reduced in size, assumes a position below rather than in front of the braincase.

In the post-cranial skeleton, the shoulder girdle is strengthened, partially by the remarkable development of the clavicle, which serves as a strut in providing leverage and permitting free arm movement in all directions. The forelimbs are elongated, while the hindlimbs develop for strength in absorbing weight transmitted by the pelvic girdle.

The pelvis itself is modified to bear the brunt of upright

posture and contribute to balance in standing and walking. For *Homo*, further specializations appear as a result of bipedalism. Pelvic bones are strengthened and surface areas enlarged to accommodate the heavy musculature necessary for vertical stance. The human foot is an engineering marvel, designed to propel the body forward in what seems even today a uniquely remarkable manner.

Among most primates, claws have given way to flattened nails on the terminal digits of both hand and foot. Claws do occur among modern primates (notably the tree-shrews) but the development of the nail clearly reflects an evolutionary trend operating responsively to the increasing importance of the grasping function and the progressive development toward tactility in the digital pads. Closely related, of course, is the evolution of a complex nerve network which lends high sensitivity to these pads.

The Fossil Primates

Our interest in the early fossil history of the primates is guided initially by our curiosity about man's beginnings. We have classed him as a primate; therefore, his present physical form is the most recent product of a long evolutionary development. The clues to this process can only be gained by investigating the fossil evidence as far back as we can find it. But what do we look for and how do we recognize ancestral forms among fossil populations that lived millions of years ago?

The answer lies simply in the preceding discussion. Keeping in mind those trends characteristic of the primate order as a whole, we look for early forms that are generalized in their physical structure rather than those that have developed certain specializations. Specializations may be represented by such structures as hooves, horns, and exaggerated proportions—long necks, long legs, or even large body size. These and other specializations represent specific adaptations to particular environmental conditions and are advantageous only so long as those conditions exist. In many cases, specialization has led to extinction. When environmental conditions change, the specialized animal does not find it easy to readapt, and may not survive in a very competitive animal world.

The generalized animal, on the other hand, has the advantage of being able to cope with changing situations. Without the limiting factors imposed by special features, it can compete and survive. Thus, anatomical generalization is our clue to ancestral relationships.

The fossil record for the primates probably begins sometime in the late Mesozoic; we say *probably* because of the inadequacy of the evidence. A few bone fragments and a few teeth are all we have to establish the earliest boundary between certain mammalian forms and the first primates. However, we know that toward the end of the Mesozoic and especially during the early epochs of the Cenozoic, the climate was warm and moist. Extensive forests covered large areas of both the Old and New Worlds—a rich habitat for the development of small tree-dwelling primates.

Although we must be satisfied with these fragmentary remains, we have been able to reconstruct a fairly good picture of the many types of primates that lived some sixty million years ago. The following examples will represent a small sample of the total. They should, however, demonstrate some feeling for the active radiation of primate forms that eventually produced our modern primates.

Fossils of the Paleocene

We cannot observe the earliest primate evidence without contemplating their ancestral relationships to other mammalian groups. Where did the primates come from? The fossil record of the Paleocene has helped to answer this question.

The most primitive primates known have been classified in the suborder *Prosimii*. They exhibit characteristics that place them in the order *Primates* but at the same time show traits that are similar to another order, *Insectivora*. We find that this mixture of traits is even more outstanding among the Paleocene fossils.

Probably the best representatives have been placed in the family *Plesiadapidae*. From a partial skeleton found in the middle Paleocene of Colorado as well as numerous jaw fragments from other North American sites, reconstructions point to an animal that is extremely close to the tree-shrew (at one time classified as an Insectivore) but having some characteristics that approach the lemur and others reminiscent of the Insectivores. One early fossil, *Anagale,* from Outer Mongolia, demonstrates a mosaic of traits suggestive of both lemur and tree-shrew. Recent analysis has placed it, at least tentatively, among the primitive tree-shrews, but this mixture of traits serves to point up the early homologous position of the two orders.

The *Plesiadapidae* varied in size from that of a squirrel to that of a house cat. They probably looked very much like rodents, with small braincases, long snouts, and large forward-slanting incisor teeth. Fossil remains from Europe have been placed in the same family; therefore *Plesiadapidae* represents one of the few primate families that lived in both the Old World and the New World. Anatomically, *Plesiadepidae* would seem to bridge the gap between certain insectivores and true primates.

Fossils of the Eocene

From their sporadic beginnings in the Paleocene, the prosimians flourished during the next epoch. They reached a developmental peak and firmly established themselves in both North America and Europe. Again, the earliest and most complete fossils come from North America. Perhaps the best-known is *Notharctus,* a lemur-like creature dating from the middle Eocene of Wyoming. *Notharctus* and the many other representatives from the New World resemble living lemurs both in their proportions and in their general structure. Also, with their shorter snouts and enlarged brains (especially in the frontal area), and stereoscopic vision, they demonstrate quite an advance over the Paleocene *Plesiadapidae*. In the Old World, examples of the Eocene prosimians are represented by the family *Adapis,* also characterized as ancient lemurs.

Another member of the *Prosimii* made its appearance during the Eocene: *Tarsiiforme,* relative of the modern tarsier. Although it is extremely difficult to differentiate between the tarsier and lemur in this early time period, two fossil families have been established to include the fragmentary remains of possible tarsioid forms: the *Anaptomorphidae* from North America and the *Tarsiidae* from Europe. Compared to the Paleocene fossils, these animals had shorter snouts and heads more upright upon the spine, as evidenced by the placement of the *foramen magnum*. Thus their skeletal anatomy suggests that they held themselves erect while hopping and sitting, much like present-day tarsiers.

Outside these two areas—North America and Europe—the prosimian record for this time period is missing. It is assumed that they must have existed elsewhere, but no evidence has been found. Of course, fossil bone quickly disintegrates under humid conditions, and the climate of Asia and Africa during Tertiary times may account for the paucity of fossil prosimian remains.

Obviously, the Eocene was an epoch of great evolutionary activity among the prosimians; fossil forms that date from the end of this period demonstrate clues to more progressive groups. *Amphipithecus* from the late Eocene deposits of Burma is a good example. A small fragment of jaw has been classified by some as a very small and primitive ape and by others as a possible cercopithecoid (Old World monkey). Wherever he belongs, *Amphipithecus* and fossils like him demonstrate the further dedevelopment of higher primate forms toward the end of the Eocene.

Fossils of the Oligocene

Oligocene deposits have yielded a fascinating sample of fossil primates. The prosimians, which reached a developmental peak during the Eocene, are found in fewer numbers. Now the cercopithecoids and pongids began to appear in a number of Old World sites.

Our earliest evidence comes from the early Oligocene deposits of western Texas. This small skull was found by Professor J. Wilson of the University of Texas and is known as *Rooneyia viejaensis*. It exhibits traits that make it a very special find. Although generally recognized as a prosimian, it has two upper premolars rather than three—the only New World primate which does—and a much more progressive brain than its prosimian colleagues of North America. In other words, it is possible that there is some ancestral relationship between *Rooneyia* in the New World and primates of the Old World, a speculation that must await further fossil evidence.

Next, we go to Egypt and to two fossil forms that come from the middle Oligocene, *Parapithecus* and *Propliopithecus.* The former is represented by a lower jaw with a full complement of teeth. This tiny creature, no larger than a present-day squirrel, exhibits a mosaic of traits that recall the prosimians (especially the tarsier) as well as the Old World monkeys and primitive apes. It is possible that *Parapithecus* (as well as *Oligopithecus,* a recent find from the same geographic area) may represent a clue to the existence of a transitional stage between the lower and higher primates.

On the other hand, the *Propliopithecus* jaw has been evaluated as an ancient gibbon-like form. This would indicate that as early as 30 million years ago, the differentiation of the pongidae had begun, producing apes that are recognizable by present-day standards.

Fossils of the Miocene and Pliocene

These two epochs have been combined because they are continuous relative to the development of the pongidae. The gibbonoid tendency initiated by the Oligocene fossil *Propliopithecus* continues throughout the last two epochs of the Tertiary. *Limnopithecus* from East Africa and *Pliopithecus* from Europe, while exhibiting traits suggestive of both monkeys and gibbons, serve to demonstrate the progressive development of the gibbon. In fact, the fossils represent the most complete paleontological record, from modern back to ancient gibbons, of any of the modern apes.

As for the remaining pongids, over twenty genera of extinct forms have been classified or recognized by various paleontologists. However, recent taxonomic revisions by Simons and Pilbeam have translated this early confusion into a simplified system, combining the late Tertiary fossil apes into three distinct genera—*Dryopithecus, Gigantopithecus,* and *Ramapithecus*—the first containing a number of species.

The fossil remains of *Dryopithecus* have been collected from both Miocene and Pliocene deposits since the middle of the nineteenth century. However, their bony inventory includes mostly teeth and jaw fragments, making total reconstruction of individuals a highly speculative project. Some generalizations can be made: their geographic range was wide, including Europe (*Dryopithecus*), Asia (*Sivapithecus*), and Africa (*Dryopithecus, Xenopithecus,* and *Proconsul*). Also, their body size was variable, from that of a modern gibbon to that of a modern gorilla.

It is difficult to characterize this large and widespread group of fossil apes, but they do have certain traits that separate them from the other late Tertiary genera. Probably the most important of these traits has to do with the arrangement of cusps, ridges, and fissures on the occlusal (biting) surfaces of the molar teeth. This characteristic is known as the *Dryopithecus pattern* or Y-5 pattern (see Figure 4) and consists of five cusps, rather than the usual four, with the fissures between the cusps

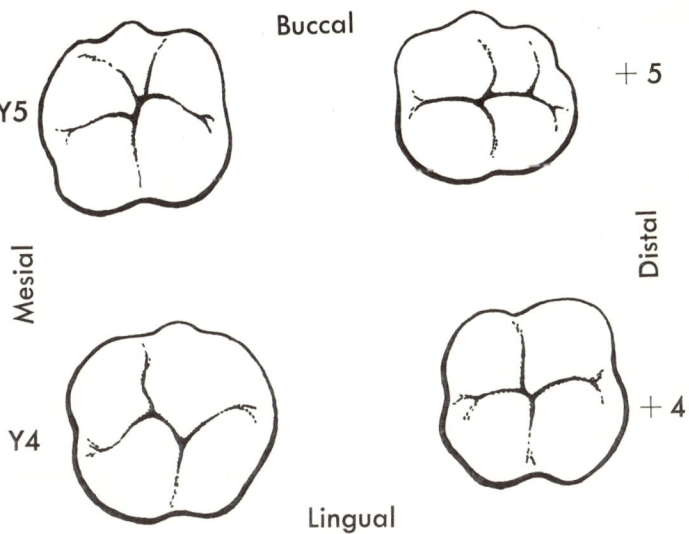

FIGURE 4 Cusp patterns for the lower molar teeth.

resembling the letter "Y." This Y-5 pattern has been demonstrated in modified form in modern pongids and in man, thus establishing the ancestral relationship between modern primates and the *Dryopithecinae*.

Our only information concerning the skull and post-cranial skeleton of *Dryopithecus* comes from East Africa, thanks to the efforts of Doctor L. S. B. Leakey. This material was originally assigned to the single genus *Proconsul* and was excavated from Rusinga Island in Lake Victoria, as well as from the nearby shores of the lake. The emergence of this material has given us a more comprehensive picture of the complete animal and the results are most interesting. *Dryopithecus* was an ape-like form that exhibited a great number of advanced cercopithecoid characteristics together with traits that suggest hominid status, particularly in the face, jaws, and dentition. Thus, in *Dryopithecus*, we have an ape whose traits demonstrate ancestor relationships to the earlier cercopithecoids and also anticipate the hominids to come later. Some authorities have seen in the remains of numerous *Dryopithecinae* evidence of terrestial rather than arboreal locomotion, as was typical for most of the primates of this time. However, on the basis of the available skeletal material—consisting primarily of teeth and jaws—it is difficult to make a definitive judgment at this time.

Gigantopithecus differs little from *Dryopithecus* except in the size of its jaws and teeth. Skeletal remains of this animal, representing a form certainly larger than our modern gorilla, have been found in both China and Northern India. *Gigantopithecus* inhabited these areas during late Pliocene and early Pleistocene times.

Again, we are frustrated by the incompleteness of the skeletal sample that represents our knowledge of *Gigantopithecus*. We have only some jaws and a number of teeth to represent this form. Larger than anything we have seen in the fossil record, this creature has been estimated by some authorities as standing some twelve feet tall. Of course, this is pure speculation, but *Gigantopithecus* is obviously the largest primate in the fossil history and seems to have become extinct sometime during the middle Pleistocene.

Perhaps the most interesting of the late Tertiary primates are the fragmentary remains that have been classified as *Rama-*

pithecus. This genus had a wide geographic range, having been found in India (*Ramapithecus, Bramapithecus*), East Africa (*Kenyapithecus*), and possibly in China.

A reconstruction of the upper jaw is remarkably human in appearance. It indicates a foreshortened face, with small incisors and short canines. It lacks the maxillary *diastema* (that gap, between lateral incisor and canine, which accommodates a projecting canine of the lower jaw and so is often termed a pongid characteristic). Also, the curve of the dental arcade is human in form.

If we were to choose one of the Miocene or Pliocene fossil primates to represent a transitional form between ape and man, certainly *Ramapithecus* would be our likeliest candidate.

In the Miocene and early Pliocene time zone, we must include a fossil group from Italy known as *Oreopithecus*. The remains of this form come from a coal mine in the Tuscany Hills of central Italy. Since their discovery almost a century ago, an abundant sample has been collected and studied by *Johannes Hurzeler,* a Swiss paleontologist.

Oreopithecus is described as a large ape, about the size of a modern chimpanzee. Rather than the long snoutlike face of Dryopithecus, *Oreopithecus* has a short, flat face. Studies of the pelvic and extremity bones indicate the possibility that *Oreopithecus* walked erect. It would seem, in fact, that *Oreopithecus* has most of the characteristics that would qualify him as a direct ancestor to the hominid family. However, recent studies, especially of the dentition, have placed this creature outside the pongid-hominid developmental line, and it is now believed that *Oreopithecus* apparently became extinct by the end of the Pliocene.

In the history of the Tertiary primates, we would expect great variability and differentiation. It is during this period that the primates reached a developmental peak. Many types and sizes of apes inhabited most areas of the Old World. However, following the Pliocene, their numbers began to decrease, and many groups met extinction. Today we are left with a mere scattering of representatives: the gibbon, orangutan, chimpanzee, and gorilla. But it is to these variable populations of the later Tertiary that our present-day primates owe their existence.

Although we have concentrated on the fossil record of the

Old World, it should be noted that primate evolution was continuing in the New World. However, it culminated in the production and further development of the Ceboidea, or New World monkeys. As far as we can tell, their appearance is relegated to the Miocene and is based on inferences drawn from specimens found in South America, notably *Homunculus* and *Cebupithecia*. The characteristics of these forms are closely related to those of living New World monkeys. Fossil pongids have not been found in the Americas; therefore, we eliminate the New World from consideration as the birthplace of man.

Summary

The epochs of the Tertiary were characterized by the early development and continued radiation of the primates. The small arboreal prosimians with their genetic foundations among the Insectivores of the Cretaceous (late Mesozoic) probably gave rise to both the Old and the New World monkeys, while some form of the former is responsible for the efflorescence of the Miocene and Pliocene pongids.

Despite the many gaps in the fossil record and the existing taxonomic confusion, we can partially reconstruct a fairly good picture of primate evolution during the Tertiary. We have representatives that anticipate our living primates; aberrant forms that in all probability represent evolutionary experiments and thus did not last long enough to play a significant role in the ancestral background of living forms; and, last but not least, fossil primates that very possibly represent ancient ancestral populations of the Pleistocene hominids.

Suggested Readings

Biegert, J.
1963. The evaluation of characteristics of the skull, hands, and feet for primate taxonomy. *In:* S. L. Washburn (ed.) *Classification and Human Evolution*, pp. 116–45. Viking Fund Publs. Anthrop., No. 37. Chicago: Aldine Publishing Company.

Clark, W. E. le Gros
1962. *The Antecedents of Man* (2d ed.). Edinburgh: Universty of Edinburgh Press.

Hofer, H. O., and J. A. Wilson
1967. An endocranial cast of an early Oligocene primate. *Folia primat.* 5:148–52.

Simons, Elwyn L.
1963. Some fallacies in the study of hominid phylogeny. *Science 141*, No. 3584:879–89.

———
1964. The early relatives of man. *Scientific American 211*, No. 1:50–62.

——— and Pilbeam, D. R.
1965. Preliminary revision of the Dryopithecinae (Pongidae, Anthropoidea). *Folia primat.* 3:81–152.

FOSSIL MAN

chapter
7

One of the frustrations inherent in the study of a new science is the maze of unfamiliar terms that inevitably confronts the beginning student. Unfortunately, physical anthropology is no exception, particularly in the case of terminology assigned to the many fossil finds. Most of these terms are lengthy and technical, often difficult to pronounce. And they are subject to constant revision, resulting in confusion not only to the student but often to the experts themselves!

Of course, there are special rules governing the naming of paleontological evidence. These rules, established by the International Code of Zoological Nomenclature, exist to assure coherent terminology, to avoid duplication, and to lend a functional nomenclature to new discoveries. Ideally, a scientific name should be in itself a statement of relationship.

In reality, however, the rules are not always followed. Early attempts to name fossil remains were handicapped by the lack of comparative material—no matter how small or fragmentary the sample may have been, it had to be considered as representative of an ancient population. Later, when more material was made available, the sample would be renamed. Today, responsible experts tend to withhold assignment of official nomenclature until a fossil is thoroughly examined and tested, but years may elapse before adequate material has accumulated to devise a systematic classification. Thus we learn to refer to a particular fossil on the basis of its geographical location (e.g., the "Swartkrans pelvis") or its discoverer (e.g., "Wilson's prosimian") until we are more reliably convinced of the material's significance and place in our scheme of things.

Nomenclature Systems

Early geologists, unaided by the relative wealth of material available today, labeled fossil remains without regard to future difficulties. By 1925, however, sufficient fossil evidence had been collected to necessitate the initiation of some grouping system, and numerous classifications were suggested to eliminate troublesome duplications and errors. One early system, for example, divided all known evidence into three classes on the basis of morphological similarity. Fossils which could not be considered hominid were termed *Protoanthropic,* "preman"; ancient representatives of man were called *Paleoanthropic,* and recent remains were termed *Neoanthropic,* or "new man." This system helped to sort out existing material but was obviously an oversimplification and did not take into account those forms which combined both modern and primitive characteristics.

Today, when a fossil is found and identified, it is generally assigned two names, one generic and one specific (e.g., *Australopithecus africanus*). In the case of very close morphological relationship, a subspecies designation may be added (e.g., *Homo sapiens sapiens* and *Homo sapiens neanderthalensis*). The only standard tool used in the classification of the early hominids, however, is the binomial nameplate.

The system utilized by most modern experts is represented below:

Genus	Species	Subspecies
Homo	sapiens	sapiens
Homo	sapiens	neanderthalensis
Homo	erectus	
Australopithecus	africanus	
Australopithecus	robustus	

This system also represents an attempt at simplicity, but it is based upon a better knowledge of the fossil evidence as a whole. There are many ways of combining and classifying the fossil hominids, and we cannot say that the above-noted system is the best or that it will remain in use indefinitely. However, it fulfills the two basic requirements for acceptability: it (1) meets with general adoption for general and common use, and (2) is consonant with existing evidence of phylogenetic relationships.

In the following pages, we will review the available fossil evidence. As we do so, we should keep in mind the difficulties in devising systems of classification and in properly placing within these systems the fossil evidence as it comes to light. Further, we must remember that we will encounter numerous questions which cannot, at present, be answered. Many fossils fit easily within the existing taxonomic framework; others seem to fit nowhere at all. We would like to be able to place all the evidence into its proper niche. Science is, after all, supposed to provide the answers. Today, however, we are able only to provide the questions. The following must therefore not be considered a final summation of our specific history, because that history as we know it today is subject to rigorous reevaluation and revision tomorrow. We present a summary of the *present* evidence, the varied interpretations of this evidence, and some educated speculations based on what little we have with which to reconstruct the early history of man.

Differentiation of Hominids and Pongids

As we have seen, man is grouped together with the apes in the superfamily *Hominoidea* on the basis of their close morphological similarities. Man, of course, shares with the pongids numerous important similarities, but he *differs* from the apes in many other characteristics. In searching for the earliest representatives of true man, it is with those differences that we are concerned. It is often difficult, when examining a fossil form—which in all probability was excavated in fragmentary condition—to distinguish between ape and man. It is often impossible to do so. We find ourselves facing our own initial question: *What is man?*

Most authorities have accepted Oakley's definition of man as a tool-making creature; that is, true man is represented by a form possessing the intellectual capacity for manufacturing tools. Numerous experts have attacked Oakley's criterion on the grounds that other primates are known to have fashioned crude tools. The chimpanzees, for example, use twigs and leaves as food-gathering implements, and we have recently learned of other isolated incidences of tool-use even among nonprimates. The tool-making criterion has therefore been modified: true man is capable of fashioning *patterned* tools for his use in food-gathering or defense.

Unless tools are excavated in clear association with skeletal remains, however, how are we to know if a questionable form represents man or ape? We look then to certain morphological criteria characteristic of each. Most of these criteria are relative; because of the close relationship of man and ape, we expect many similarities. We must be able to determine, preferably through scientific measurement—but often necessarily through subjective judgment following careful consideration—whether these criteria are reliable. For example, brain capacity was long considered an excellent indication that man was—or was not—represented by a particular fossil form. However, a large brain relative to total body weight is characteristic of both ape and man. It is true that the brain capacity of modern man surpasses that of modern ape, but we cannot set an absolute numerical value which will separate man (modern or ancient) from his primate relatives. Table III presents some of the similar morphological traits used, in the relative sense, to distinguish hominid from pongid in the fossil record.

Limb proportions are examined: generally we expect the forelimbs of an ape to exceed his hindlimbs in length, while the opposite is true for man, due to the modifications inherent in his assumption of erect bipedal locomotion. We will note additional factors as we examine the fossil evidence for the evolution of man.

We should note here that numerous attempts have been made to assess taxonomic status *quantitatively*—that is, through a bio-

TABLE III

Morphological Traits used to Differentiate Early Hominid and Pongid Fossils

Trait	Hominid	Pongid
Forehead	present & high	absent
Brows	small	large
Nose	jutting bridge	no bridge
Canine tooth	nonprojecting	large, projecting
Dental arcade	parabolic	U-shaped
Chin	present	absent
Foramen magnum	placed near center of skull base	placed at back of skull base

metrical evaluation of characters. The difficulties involved are obvious: no one is able to determine reliably the relative importance of each observed feature. Not all morphological characters are equally relevant. Further, such an approach precludes the evaluation of a total morphological pattern, which, as we have seen, is a crucial observation in determining phylogenetic relationships.

The Australopithecines

In 1925, Professor Raymond Dart described a skull excavated from deposits in the Transvaal of South Africa, which he named *Australopithecus*. The skull, incorporating hominid and pongid traits, aroused great interest. Within ten years, other discoveries from the same region followed. The finds were exciting, and —as could be expected—the interpretations were varied and controversial.

Most of the fossil evidence that represents the genus *Australopithecus* was literally blasted from a number of caves. Through the combined efforts of Professor Dart and Dr. Robert Broom, the skeletal fragments of a large number of individuals were collected.

As the skeletal inventory grew and more sites were recognized, it became obvious to most experts that the evidence indicated more than a single population. The reconstructed forms from

Kromdraai and Swartkrans were larger and more robust than those from Taungs, Sterkfontein, and Makapansgat. Thus the decision was made to recognize two species: *Australopithecus robustus* and *Australopithecus africanus,* which, on the basis of new dating techniques, dated from approximately two million years.

A. robustus not only includes the material from South Africa but, if some authorities are correct, is represented in eastern Africa (in the remains of *Zinjanthropus boisei*) and in Java (in the remains termed *Meganthropus paleojavanicus*). The incorporation of the forms found outside South Africa would mean that the species could be dated from Early Pleistocene through Middle Pleistocene, an exceedingly long period of time as well as an expansive geographical distribution.

A. robustus individuals were physically more "ape-like" in many anatomical features than *A. africanus.* Briefly, they featured greater facial protrusion, larger brow ridges, larger mandibles, and more rugged muscle attachment areas. Hominid characters, however, are represented also, particularly in the dentition—most emphatically not of the typical pongid type—and in the skeletal anatomy of the lower extremities and pelvis, which suggest that *robustus* stood and walked erect. This puzzling combination of pongid and hominid traits makes it difficult to classify these individuals as either ape-like men or man-like apes. As yet, there is general agreement that these creatures did not manufacture bone or stone tools, a consensus which by the historical criterion would deny them hominid status. Dietary implications suggest no concentration of meat, but a probable regular diet of roots, nuts, and fruit.

A. africanus represents an early form much closer to what we think of as an ancestral type for modern man (see Figure 5). Compared to *robustus, africanus* is more gracile, or delicate. *Africanus* was small, reaching an average stature of approximately 5'7". Like *robustus,* he walked erect. The brow ridges, so pronounced in *robustus,* were small, and the cranium, or skull vault, was smoother, lacking the large bony attachment areas so necessary for the great muscularity of *robustus.*

Brain size in *africanus* was small, averaging an approximate five hundred cubic centimeters, which compares favorably with modern-day gorillas. However, brain topography was much more complicated than in any living ape, and the frontal lobes were larger; in the evolution of man, changes in brain structure are more indicative of phylogenetic development than simple brain size.

From dentition studies, *africanus* appears to have maintained a higher protein diet than *robustus*. *Africanus* was essentially a meat-eater.

Geographic distribution is predominantly South African, but this conclusion rests primarily on the lack of skeletal evidence from other parts of the world rather than a true knowledge of possible ancient migration.

Here we have two populations that demonstrate a mosaic of hominid and pongid physical characteristics and who lived over a million years ago. Just where do we place them in the developmental history of modern man? Numerous authors have identified the Australopithecines as an evolutionary stage between the variable Tertiary pongids and a more developed type that made its appearance later in the Middle Pleistocene. Of the two populations, *africanus* has more supporters for this transitional-stage hypothesis than does *robustus*, which has generally been relegated to the status of an aberrant form, eventually becoming extinct.

Certainly, considering their intermediate morphology and early date, this interpretation of the *A. africanus* population has much merit. However, we find that attempts to interpret the complex character of the Australopithecines almost equal the number of scholars who write about them. We do know that these South African groups must have played a relevant role in the phylogenetic history of man. Just what that role was must rest with evidence produced by future investigators.

Problem Cases

The story of the Australopithecines is complicated by two fossil forms, *Homo habilis* and *Telanthropus capensis*. In the paleontological record of the hominids, nothing is simple; the more evidence we accumulate, the more puzzling the story becomes.

Homo habilis is the stepchild of Dr. L. S. B. Leakey and was found at his famous site in the Olduvai Gorge in Tanzania, East Africa. The fragmentary remains represent skeletal por-

AUSTRALOPITHECUS

FIGURE 5 *Australopithecus* is known to us by a variety of forms. *Robustus* was aberrant and doomed to extinction. But the morphologically advanced *Africanus,* reconstructed here, may represent an important early step in the trek from ape to man. His skull, shown above right, demonstrates a large cranial capacity for the time-span occupied, represented at right by the time-wheel. The search for more remains continues across Africa and Asia, but so far—with the single exception of the suspected Java find—all sites are confined to Africa. *Photo courtesy of Douglas H. Smith, Austin, Texas.*

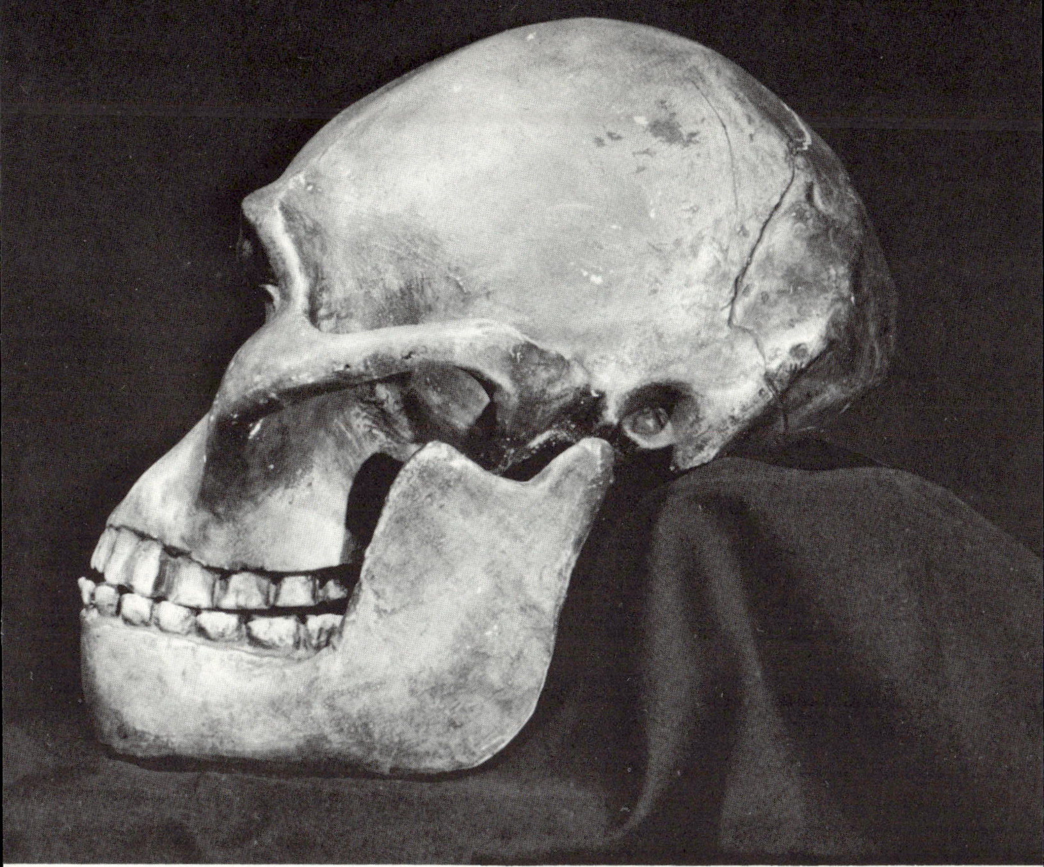

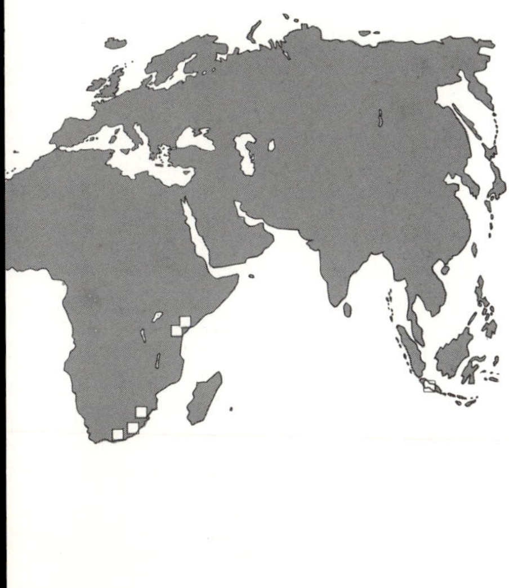

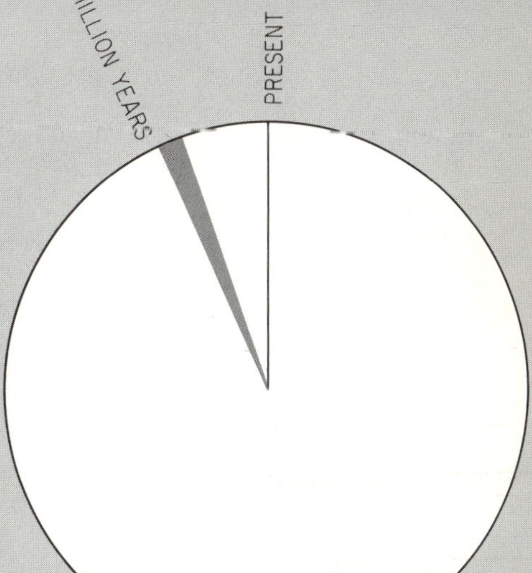

tions of numerous individuals that seem to demonstrate a more modern morphology than *Australopithecus* but not so much so that they may be included in the next taxonomic grouping, *Homo erectus*. *Habilis* remains suggest an extremely short population, almost pygmoid, with an estimated cranial capacity of approximately 680 cc and upright stance.

Leakey believes that this material represents an independent hominid population contemporary with *Australopithecus*. He believes further that *habilis* is responsible for the manufacture of the pebble tools found throughout South and East Africa (designated *Pre-Chelles-Acheul*). Others are not eager to accept Leakey's views. Many see the *habilis* sample as an advanced representative of *A. africanus,* on its phylogenetic way toward producing the next hominid stage in human evolution. A general meeting of the minds is not immediately evident. Again, we wait for further developments.

Telanthropus capensis had its beginnings in the inventive mind of Dr. Robert Broom. The site at Swartkrans had produced a number of individuals now classified as *A. robustus*. Two mandibles, the proximal end of a tibia, and other fragments were discovered in the same area but were not characteristic of *robustus*. Morphologically, these remains indicate a much smaller individual than *robustus,* with many more modern characteristics, seeming to represent a morphology typical in much more recent times. The taxonomic position of *Telanthropus,* of course, is under re-evaluation. Many experts have determined that it properly belongs with *Homo erectus,* to be discussed in the next section. Others would assign it to *Australopithecus.* Until general agreement is reached, it remains a problem case.

The question that arises is whether or not we have evidence of a true hominid form associated with the more primitive *Australopithecus,* in itself an exciting speculation. But again, the paucity of evidence for *capensis* makes any hasty decision impossible.

Homo Erectus

The present fossil evidence indicates that, by the beginning of the second interglacial, true hominids had spread over most of the Old World. Skeletal samples of their existence have been found in Java (*Pithecanthropus erectus*, found by Dubois and von Koenigswald), in China (*Sinanthropus pekinensis* by Black and Weidenreich), in northwest Africa (*Atlanthropus mauritanicus* by Arambourg), and in East Africa (*Chellean III* by Leakey). If a recent discovery from Vertesszöllös, Hungary, is accepted as *Homo erectus,* then eastern Europe may be added to the geographical distribution of this species.

By lumping all of these populations into the same genus and species, *Homo erectus,* we have not only simplified the taxonomic situation but also have automatically revealed the true evolutionary position for each of the remains. In other words, the grouping was made for sound reasons, after careful examination and comparison. The populations noted all date from approximately the same time period—early mid-Pleistocene—and they demonstrate numerous morphological similarities.

From what we have learned from the skeletal remains of *Homo erectus,* we are able to picture him as a short (averaging a little over five feet), powerful individual with a well-developed upright posture. The stamp of his pongid ancestry is obvious, particularly in the skull (see Figure 6). We might say that from an evolutionary standpoint, the post-cranial skeleton of early man developed faster toward modern standards than did the skull. The *erectus* cranium is small, with an average capacity of about one thousand cc, with a very low crown and no forehead. The brow-ridges are massive, the face broad with large, round orbits, the nose short and broad, and there is no chin.

We assume that all the known representatives of *homo erectus* made tools and knew how to use fire, but our best evidence of this comes from China and Africa. In China, at the famous site of Choukoutien, we find large hearths and charred bone. Also, crude core tools termed *choppers* are found extensively throughout the site. In Africa, the tools are somewhat more sophisticated in that the core tools are bifacially chipped hand-axes.

Some *erectus* groups may have been cannibalistic. We have found skulls with their basilar portions removed, presumably in an attempt to reach the brains, and split long bones, suggesting a forage for marrow. Whether *Homo erectus* individuals feasted on each other or were eaten by outsiders is a question we cannot answer at this time.

HOMO ERECTUS

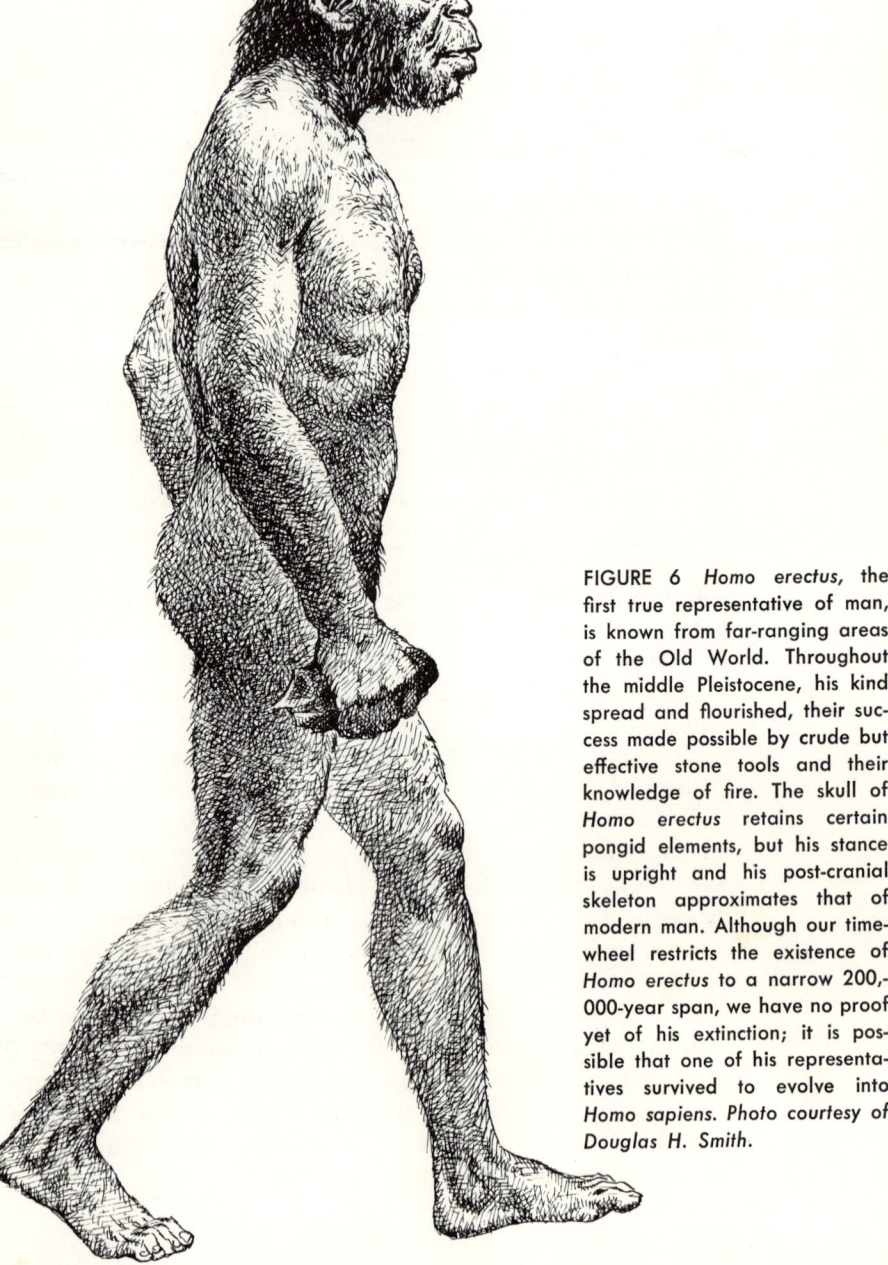

FIGURE 6 *Homo erectus*, the first true representative of man, is known from far-ranging areas of the Old World. Throughout the middle Pleistocene, his kind spread and flourished, their success made possible by crude but effective stone tools and their knowledge of fire. The skull of *Homo erectus* retains certain pongid elements, but his stance is upright and his post-cranial skeleton approximates that of modern man. Although our time-wheel restricts the existence of *Homo erectus* to a narrow 200,-000-year span, we have no proof yet of his extinction; it is possible that one of his representatives survived to evolve into *Homo sapiens. Photo courtesy of Douglas H. Smith.*

500,000
0
PRESENT
500,000
YEARS

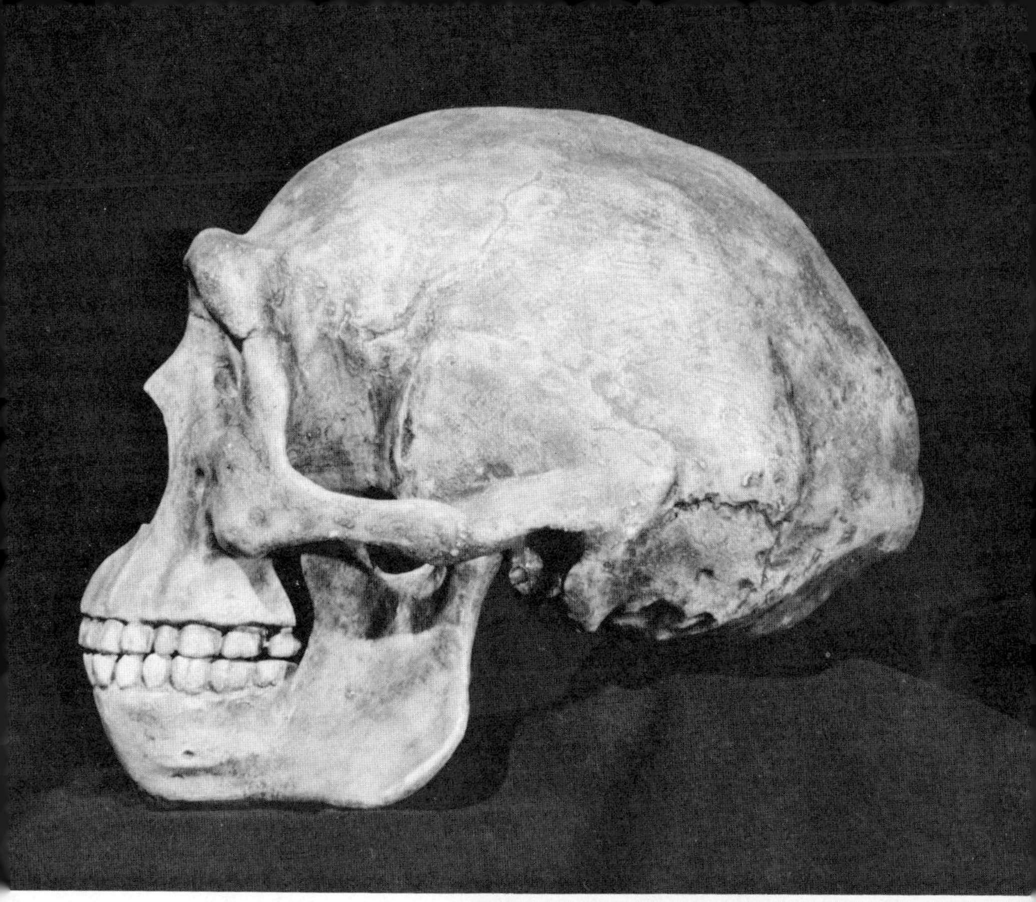

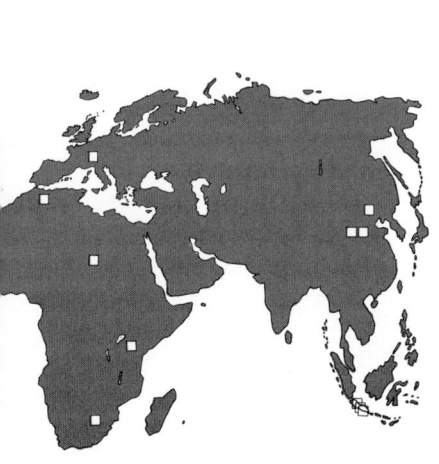

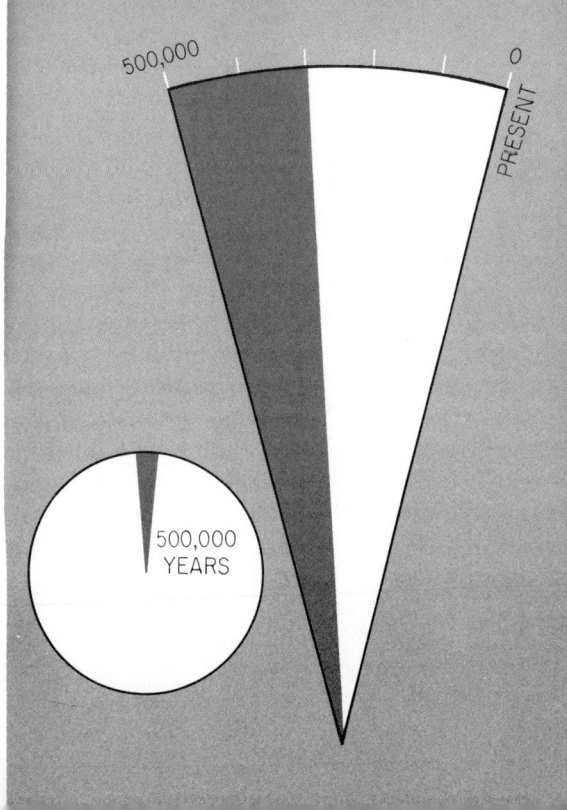

Clues to the origins of *Homo erectus* come from Africa and possibly Java. Both *Australopithecus* and *Homo erectus* are found in Africa and the possibility that *A. africanus* is ancestral to *erectus* is strongly suggested. Also, one of the earliest finds on the island of Java, a small fragment of mandible (*Meganthropus paleojavanicus*), looks to some experts like *Australopithecus* in Java. At the very least, this is an interesting speculation and an example of the efforts expended toward a most important function of physical anthropology: the interpretation of data through time and space. The fragmentary remains unearthed from early deposits provide bits and pieces of a long and fascinating history; it is up to the physical anthropologist to total them up, to fit them together in such a way that with time we are able to reconstruct with some certainty the history of our species.

Homo Sapiens Neanderthalensis

In 1856, quarry workers in the Neander Valley of Germany uncovered some ancient bones that were hastily discarded since they had nothing to do with the job at hand. By a fortunate but circuitous route, these bones eventually fell into the hands of Hermann Schaaffhausen, a professor at Heidelberg University. He identified the fossil bones as human but belonging to a very primitive race. The good professor had a difficult time persuading his knowledgeable colleagues of the nature and importance of his discovery; most of his peers agreed that the remains represented a pathological monster of some kind. However, over the years similar monsters were found throughout the Old World and became known as the Neanderthals, a population later to become extremely important in the evolutionary saga of man.

It is almost as if the Neanderthals had wanted us to know them, for we are favored with remains in numbers unsurpassed by other early populations. They were the first to bury their dead, filling shallow graves with tools and food. They lived primarily in caves and hunted the large herbivores and carnivores of their time.

The Neanderthals represent a highly variable population that left their mark in most of the geographic areas of the Old World. From the best-described skeleton taken from the rock shelter of La Chapelle, France, to the zinc mine at Broken Hill in Rhodesia and the cave known as Skhul in Palestine, we must consider this population in all of its varieties as well as its role in the complicated course of human evolution.

Figures 7, 8, and 9 may help to emphasize the different kinds of Neanderthals that populated the Old World over a time span from the third interglacial to the middle of the first interstadial of the Würm glaciation.

First, the Neanderthal from western Europe and Iraq (at Shanidar)—these representatives (see Figure 7) have been categorized as typical or Classic. They are short, squat (a little over five feet tall), and extremely robust. In some ways they are more robust examples of *Homo erectus,* but there are important differences. Their skulls, although very low and long, are huge. Cranial capacities climb over 1600 cc in numerous specimens, a figure well over the average cranial capacity for modern man. Brow-ridges are huge, with large round orbits. The faces, very long, feature fairly extensive prognathism, rugged lower jaws, and little or no chin. Heavily muscled, barrel-chested individuals, the Neanderthals seem to have been sufficiently resourceful to deal with whatever problems their environment imposed.

In Africa, we find a variety that is certainly reminiscent of the European and Middle Eastern type but with some very important differences. Although robust and short, the Neanderthal from Rhodesia (Figure 8) and Saldanha, on the coast of southeast Africa, has a much smaller skull (about 1200 cc) and exhibits brow-ridges that rival those of the modern gorilla. Also, the face is narrower and much longer than that of his European cousins.

From Palestine we find another variety of Neanderthal. Extracted from the Skhul Cave (Figure 9) are a number of individuals that demonstrate a more refined Neanderthal. These have been termed Progressive Neanderthals. The cranium is not so large as the European specimen (about 1400 cc) but the brow-ridges are smaller, the facial area more vertical, and the prognathism so typical of the other Neanderthals much reduced. In other words, although we have classified this population from

NEANDERTHAL MAN

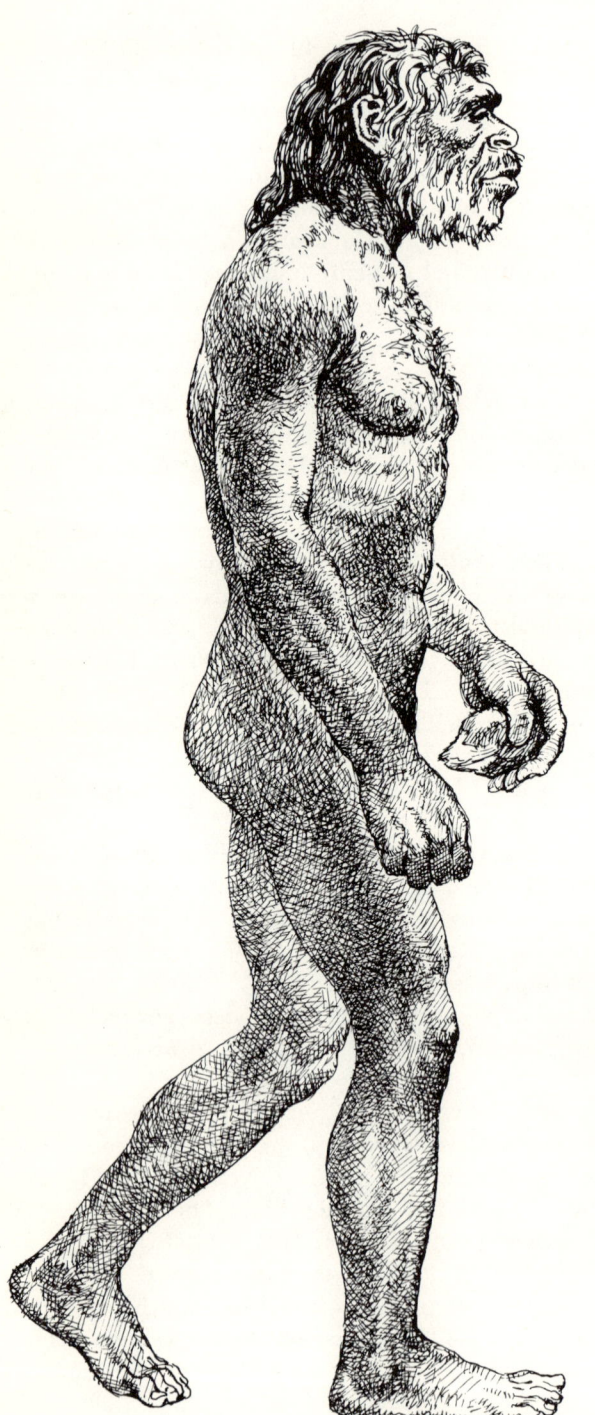

FIGURE 7 The best known of all fossil men, the Neanderthals represent a highly variable population that ranged throughout the Old World. Remains dating from 100,000 to 40,000 years before present, found in association with a well-developed cultural assembly, point to a form so similar to modern man that we place it in our own species. Indeed, should a representative of Neanderthal be dropped into our present-day world, he would go unnoticed except as a rather rugged specimen of *Homo sapiens sapiens*. Neanderthal Man, as reconstructed at left and photographed at right, is typical for the population in Europe. *Photo courtesy of Douglas H. Smith.*

500,000
0
PRESENT
500,000
YEARS

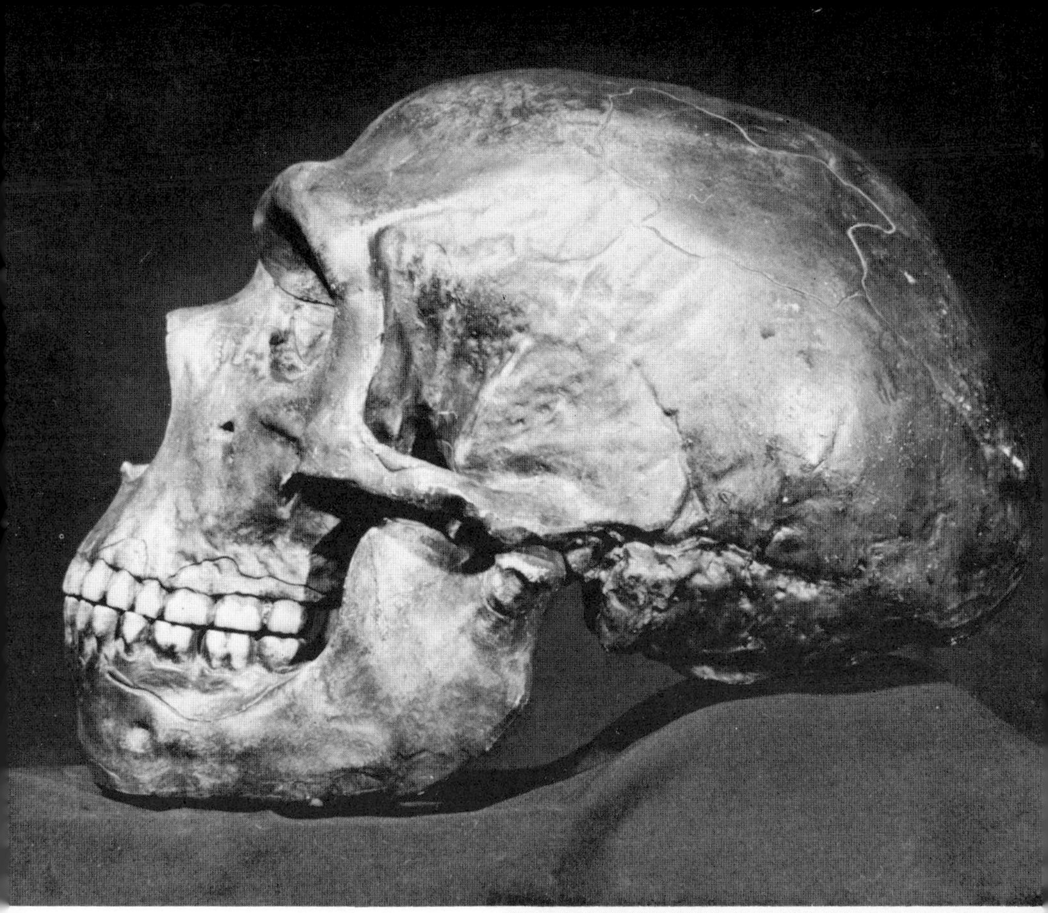

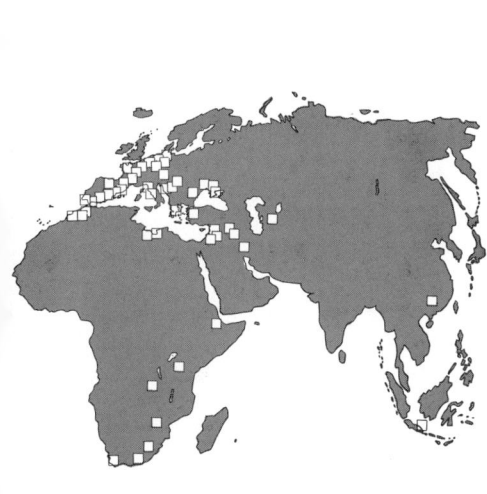

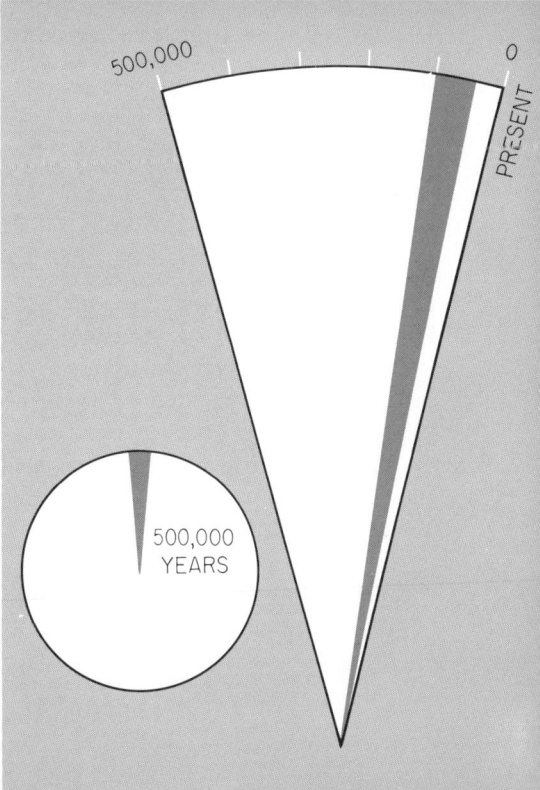

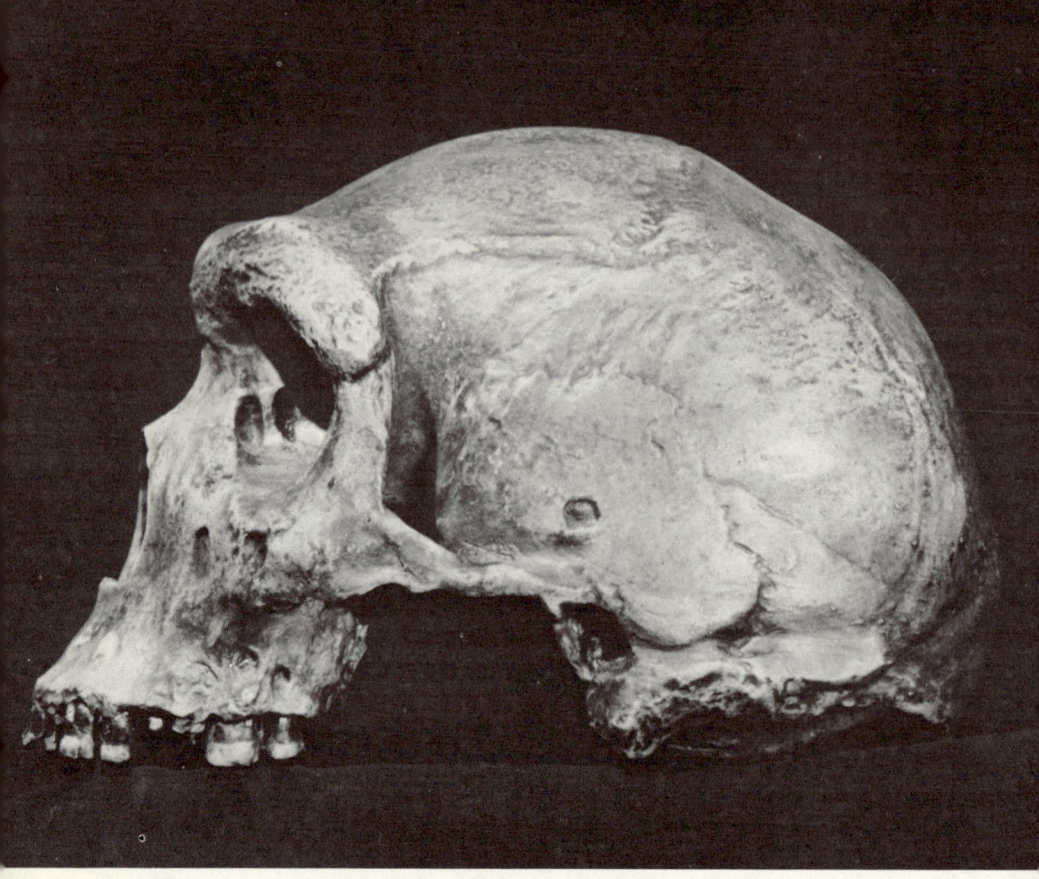

FIGURE 8 *Homo sapiens neanderthalensis*, represented here by a cast of the Rhodesian skull from Broken Hill, Rhodesia, South Africa, demonstrates the African variety of Neanderthal. His skull is smaller, the face longer. More pronounced brow ridges lend a more rugged appearance. See Figure 7 for placement in time-scale, geographical distribution, and illustration of the reconstructed man. *Photo courtesy of Douglas H. Smith.*

Palestine as Neanderthal, they exhibit physical characteristics that anticipate a more advanced morphology. Physical variation is the rule for *neanderthalensis.*

Did the Neanderthals represent a stage in the developmental history of modern man, or were they an aberrant form that found extinction during the last fluctuations of the Würm glaciation, leaving no record of their genetic existence among the living populations of today? Again, we have questions and no answers. Both possibilities have been tenaciously defended,

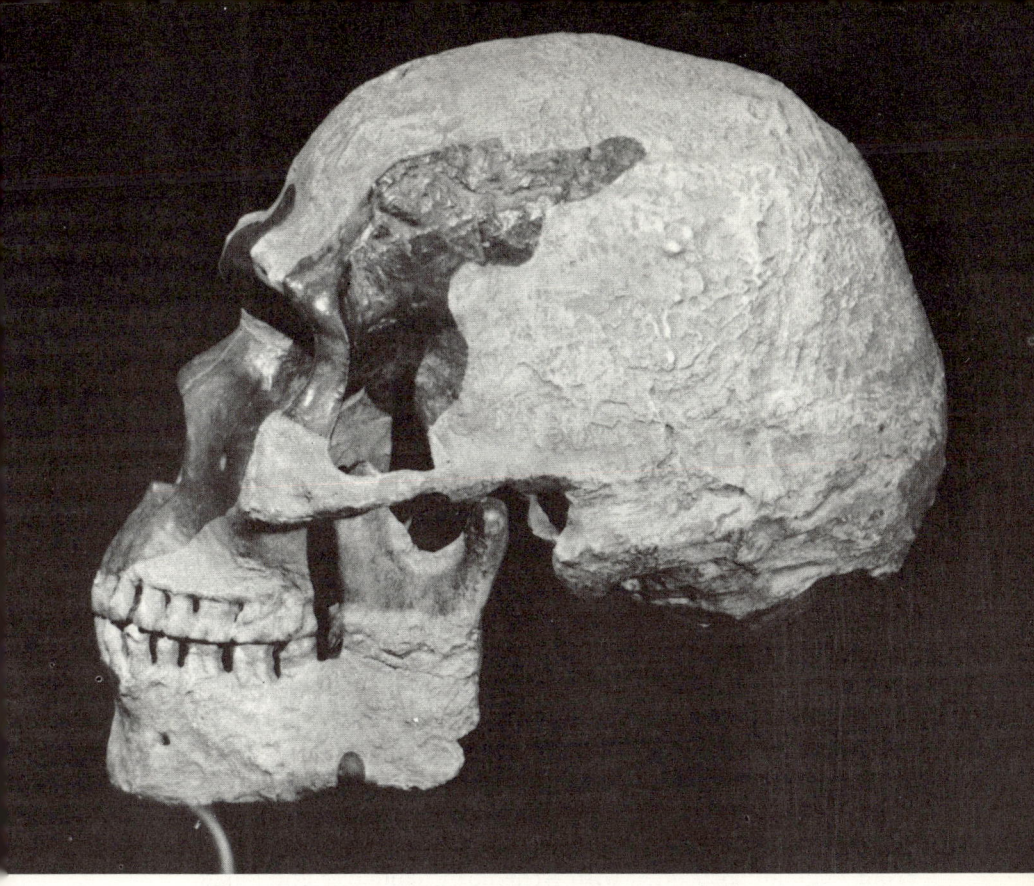

FIGURE 9 *Homo sapiens neanderthalensis,* from Skhul Cave at Mt. Carmel, Palestine. Neanderthal in the Middle East is progressive: he appears more modern, more closely resembling modern man. Note the higher skull vault, with brow ridges and prognathism less pronounced, and the well-developed chin. See Figure 7 for placement in time-scale, geographical distribution, and illustration of the reconstructed man. *Photo courtesy of Douglas H. Smith.*

while some authors divide the Neanderthals into *Classic* (Spy, La Chapelle, La Quina, Shanidar) and *Progressive* (Krapina, Ehringsdorf, Skhul) varieties. The hypothesis is that only the Classics traveled the road to extinction, whereas the Progressives, with their combination of archaic and modern traits, were directly ancestral to *Homo sapiens sapiens.* The choices are many and interpretations shift as the evidence grows. Man's evolutionary history is filled with many blanks, but speculation, based on available evidence, is the name of the game.

Problem Cases

Complicating the many attempts to interpret the phylogenetic position of the Neanderthals are a number of fossil forms that must be considered at length. A brief description of these fossils should help to demonstrate what we mean.

HEIDELBERG

Found by Otto Schoetensack and named after a city in Germany, this find is represented by a large mandible (Figure 10) only. This lower jaw is large and rugged and first impressions indicate a Neanderthal morphology. However, its geological date is late first interglacial, much earlier than any of the recognized Neanderthals and occupying a time period that we have relegated to *Homo erectus*. Some claim that Heidelberg represents the ancestral population of the later Neanderthals, while others see this mandible as *Homo erectus* in Europe.

SWANSCOMBE

From England, associated with Acheulean hand-axes and dated as late second interglacial, we have an individual represented only by the back portion of a skull (the occipital and two parietal bones). This isn't much to work with, but these remains have been subjected to meticulous examination. Descriptions reveal a combination of primitive (or Neanderthal) and modern features. Without a face and important post-cranial material, it is extremely difficult to associate the Swanscombe remains with either the Neanderthal or sapiens populations of Europe. The early date also adds to the problem of interpretation.

STEINHEIM

Steinheim Man, represented by a single, distorted skull, dates also from the last part of the second interglacial. Lacking mandible and any association with cultural artifacts, its early date intrigues anthropologists, who have at various times classified it as *Homo sapiens* and as *Homo Neanderthalensis*. The skull

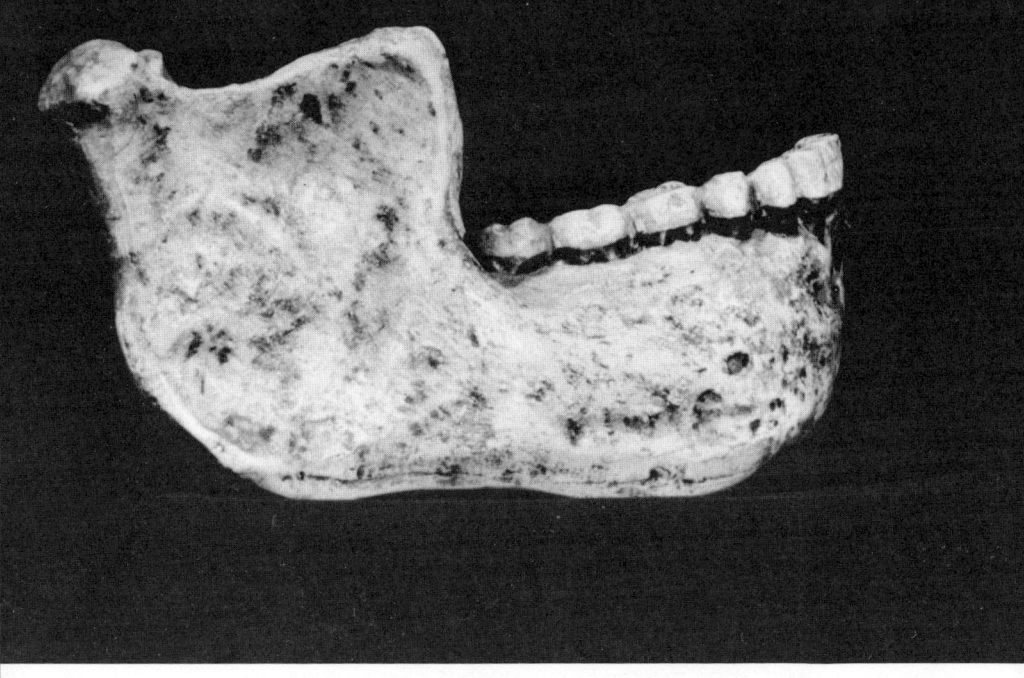

FIGURE 10 Reproduction of the Heidelberg mandible. Photo courtesy of Douglas H. Smith.

is thick, the brow-ridges pronounced; clearly Steinheim is an intermediate form. If it is related to Swanscombe—as some authorities suggest—it may represent a widely spread population of proto-modern men. See Figure 11.

FONTECHEVADE

A similar problem find comes from the Fontechevade site in France. Again, we are faced with an early date, third interglacial, and a paucity of skeletal remains. Actually, there are two individuals represented: portions of the skull top of one and a corner of the frontal bone of another. With the exception of the bones' thickness, all characteristics are modern. Most authors have classified these remains as *Homo sapiens sapiens* but dating from earlier times than any other sapiens known in

EARLY HOMO SAPIENS

FIGURE 11 The earliest forms representing *Homo sapiens* come from sites in Europe: at Steinheim, Montmaurin, and Swanscombe. The skull shown at right demonstrates the appearance of a form incorporating both modern and Neanderthaloid traits—more than 100,000 years before the first Neanderthal. Skeletal evidence is scanty, but sufficient for the reconstruction, at left, of the Steinheim remains, believed to be the immediate successor to *Homo erectus* in Europe. *Photo courtesy of Douglas H. Smith.*

500,000
0
PRESENT
500,000
YEARS

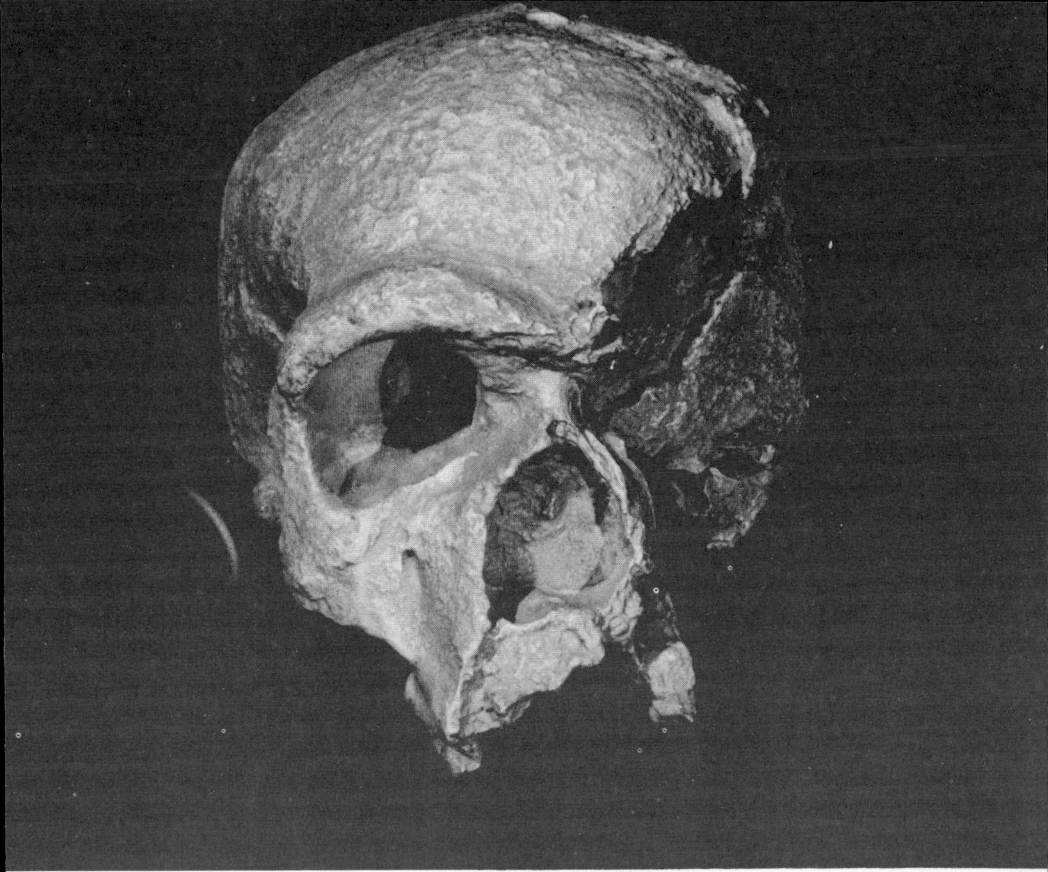

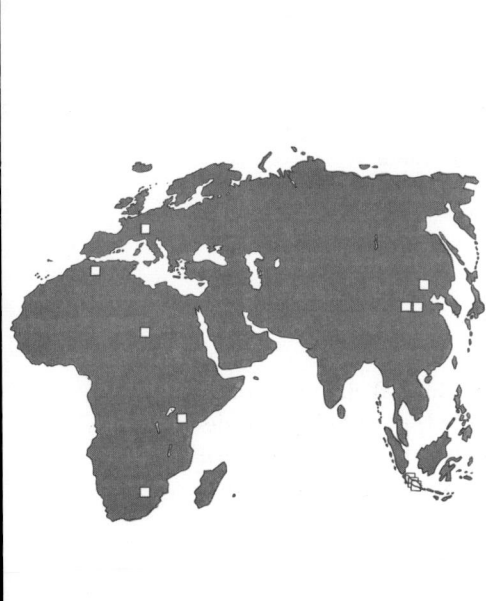

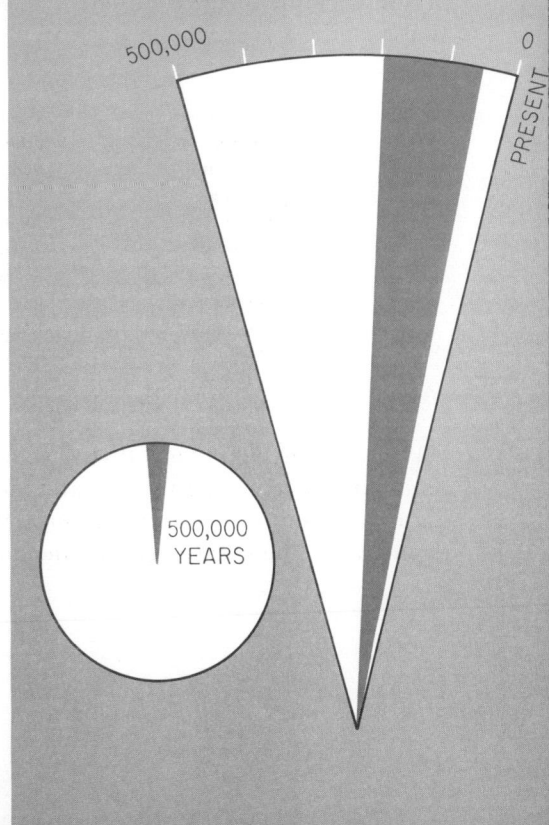

Europe. We have yet to account conclusively for these heavy, thick, but modern remains.

The early date and morphological mixture of these four finds, then, makes their placement in the developmental history of man an extremely difficult problem to solve. Finding the missing portions of any of the three would certainly add to our knowledge and aid in our attempts to understand their true relationships.

Homo Sapiens Sapiens

At the close of the Pleistocene, the Neanderthals disappear from the fossil record. No one really knows what happened to them, but their place was taken by new populations who looked very much like modern man. These groups introduced a new morphology, new stone and bone tools, and—in some cases—an artistic development that was amazingly unique.

Homo sapiens sapiens appeared throughout the Old World in numerous groups, almost simultaneously, beginning some forty thousand years ago. The following brief list gives an idea of the geographic distribution of some of these early populations:

Cro Magnon	France
Chancelade	France
Predmost	Yugoslavia
Grimaldi	Italy
Afalou	Algeria, N. Africa
Oldoway	Tanzania, E. Africa
Boskop	South Africa
Hotu	Iran
Choukoutien	China
Wadjak	Java
Keilor	Australia

We have already stated that the individual skeletons looked very much like modern man, and detailed morphological descriptions would therefore be superfluous. Like our modern populations, these early groups demonstrated great variability.

Some authorities have pointed out that the skeletal material from a number of these sites represents our earliest evidence of racial differentiation. For example, the remains from Cro Magnon could be Caucasoid, while those from Grimaldi appear Negroid and those from Chancelade exhibit numerous Mongoloid traits. Wadjak and Keilor specimens suggest Australoid affinities. This may mean that our modern races had their origins in the variable populations of the late Pleistocene. But racial classification at a point so distant in time is difficult. Other authorities give little credence to racial interpretations of material from late Pleistocene times.

It is the ultimate responsibility of any scientist to use what evidence he has to add to the theoretical development of his field. Our interest has been human evolution; our problem, to place the variety of fossil evidence into some meaningful developmental or phylogenetic sequence that attempts to reconstruct man's physical history over the last two million years. Obviously, there are numerous ways in which to do this, but generally the interpretations can be divided into two schools of thought. One maintains that our earliest ancestors originated in several geographic areas, each area producing its own hominid forms and eventually leading to the types of people who populate that part of the world today; such an approach is termed *polyphyletic*. For example, the followers of this school of thought would say that the fossil sequence from Asia terminated in our modern Mongoloid and Australoid races. The African evidence demonstrates the development of contemporary Negroid populations.

The *monophyletic* school, on the other hand, holds that present population distributions result from a single origin site, followed by local differentiation and extensive migration. Africa is selected as the area of origin and the *Australopithecinae* as the proposed ancestral beginning. Migration and genetic differentiation produced *Homo erectus* in all the major areas of the Old World, followed by a number of radiating forms—some successful, some unsuccessful. The ultimate result was *Homo sapiens sapiens* with his wide geographical range and extensive morphological variation. Understandably, there is merit as well as valid objection to both attempts to explain the fossil record.

Conclusion

We have attempted to illustrate in this chapter the evidence of man's physical development over the last two million years. Our evidence has consisted of human skeletal material that has been extracted from the earth in most of the countries of the Old World. The general picture is one of morphological change through time, demonstrating a wide range of morphological differentiation rather than simple stages of development. Attempts to reconstruct hominid phylogeny are numerous, and we have tried not to make premature decisions regarding developmental patterns. Speculation is inherent in any science where theory grows and changes as more evidence is compiled. Certainly new fossil finds as well as more refined methodologies may solve many of the problems that have been outlined in this chapter. Man's innate curiosity about himself, his past, and his future will always keep physical anthropologists busy gathering and interpreting the data, whether on this planet or on other planets yet to be inhabited. There are worlds yet to explore, and we've barely touched the surface of this one.

Suggested Readings

Clark, W. E. LeGros
   1964. *The Fossil Evidence for Human Evolution* (2d ed.). Chicago: Univ. of Chicago Press.

   1967. *Man-apes or Ape-men?* New York: Holt, Rinehart & Winston.

Leakey, L. S. B.
   1960. *Adam's Ancestors*. New York: Harper & Row, Inc.

CULTURAL PREHISTORY

chapter
8

From the preceding chapters, we now know something about the fossil history of the human body during the last three million years. To some extent, this history gives us insight into the development of human behavior. From cranial capacity and endocranial casts of the skull, for example, we are able to glean some idea of the intellectual level of the individual or population under investigation, while the postcranial skeleton indicates posture (pronograde or orthograde) and all that posture is known to imply.

Culture and Human Behavior

In addition to the physical remains of early populations, however, we have what are often referred to as *fossils of the mind:* cultural manifestations of human behavior. We call these objects of man-made construction *artifacts*—stone tools, clothing, basketry, etc. From a careful examination of such artifacts, we can infer their purpose, the manner in which they were made and used, and—to a certain degree—the amount of intelligence involved in making them. In essence, all artifacts reflect the degree of culture or civilization possessed by the beings who manufactured them.

In building a knowledge of early populations, we are particularly concerned with artifacts found in association with human skeletal remains, and we will be primarily concerned in this section with the cultural evidence associated with the fossil populations previously under consideration (Chapter 7). Thus the timespan covered in this chapter is limited to the Pleistocene.

Unfortunately, the early representatives of ancient populations did not anticipate our eagerness to learn about the past. Some populations left behind meager skeletal remains, with no cultural evidence whatsoever, while other populations are represented through their cultural remains alone. As a result, there is a certain inadequacy in the cultural record despite the diligent efforts of the archeologists. There is, actually, no dearth of material, but this apparent wealth is hopelessly one-sided at the present time, consisting primarily of stone and bone objects. Few, if any, evidences of clothing, fabrics, skins, housing materials, basketry, or wooden articles have survived. There are, then, many blanks in our knowledge of the cultural life of early man. But, as in the case of skeletal remains, we are constantly striving to narrow the gaps as more and more material comes to light.

Stone, of course, provides the most durable indication of early cultural efforts. It is the most imperishable of all materials used by prehistoric man for the manufacture of his tools and weapons. There are many types and kinds of stone in the world, some better suited for tool-making than others. Probably the most commonly utilized are flint and obsidian (volcanic glass). Both are fine-grained and homogeneous structurally, and for these reasons are easily fractured or flaked. Where these types of stone are not found in nature, other types are utilized despite the fact that they are more difficult to work with. Among the often used coarser-grained types are quartz, quartzite, and granite.

A number of historians have argued that the nature of the available material had a great influence on the type of stone tools made by early populations. There is abundant evidence, however, to the contrary. One of the most astonishing facts revealed in the study of artifacts is the constancy of tool types irrespective of the material available.

Another erroneous but widely held view is that the making of stone tools and weapons was a slow and laborious process, the implication being that such time-consuming efforts did not matter in stone-age times since early man, unhampered by the complexities of modern civilization, had plenty of time on his hands. Such a concept of Paleolithic life is far from realistic. We must realize that early man was totally dependent for his survival on his success in hunting, trapping, and the collection of wild edible fruits. From studies made of contemporary primitive peoples, we know that such a life is not an easy one: the individuals fight a constant battle with nature, using their total time and energies in a never-ceasing struggle to wrest from an often hostile environment sufficient food supplies for sheer survival. Some Australian groups, still living culturally in the Paleolithic, provide an excellent example, as do many of the Eskimo groups.

If the making of stone implements required many hours of work, early man would have starved to death long ago, leaving no ancestors to populate the earth. To the contrary, the making of implements from stone involves a simple matter of controlling the fracture; once the basic technique is mastered, the actual making of a useful tool is a fairly rapid process. Numerous anthropologists, sufficiently interested in the technique to put themselves to the test, have found that they can produce a functional stone tool from a pointed piece of bone in a matter of moments.

The earliest stone tools, of course, are hardly comparable to the arrow points we like to collect today. Many are, at least to the untrained eye, barely touched nodules of stone, and the question arises of how to distinguish primitive man-made artifacts from tool-like forms produced by some natural process. Actually, there are few natural conditions which offer the opportunity for the production of a stone flake that appears man-made. Prehistoric man manufactured flakes from a stone core by *percussion* (striking one stone against another) or by *pressure* (literally squeezing off small flakes with the help of a pointed bone tool).

Under certain conditions, flakes may result from natural causes, such as in rapidly moving streams, when flakes are formed as the result of stones hitting against one another. However, the production of a flake which will genuinely simulate a manmade flake by percussion involves (1) a follow-through blow, (2) the correct amount of force relative to resistance, and (3) the correct direction of the blow. Unless all three conditions are simultaneously met, the flakes resulting from accidental collision cannot be mistaken for human workmanship.

The same may be said for flakes produced as a result of natural pressure. Geologic deposits are subject to all kinds of movement. Rocks rub together to produce flakes through such pressure, but the results cannot be mistaken for those produced by human craftsmanship. Early man sharpened his stone tools by pressuring off small flakes from the working edges of his tools. This secondary retouching can be duplicated by natural forces, but because of the haphazard pattern of the scars left by the removal of the flakes, deliberate manufacture is easily recognized.

Bone tools are also subject to identification. Often, buried bone is attacked by small rodents, their gnawing occasionally producing a tool-like form. Small parallel grooves made by rodent teeth, however, are apparent and easily distinguished from human retouching. Further, a bone tool generally exhibits a surface gloss, resulting from constant use; this gloss cannot be duplicated under the usual natural conditions.

As stone is the most durable material used by early man, the ancient cultures are classified on the basis of stone implements recovered from sites of early habitation. In cultural prehistory, we utilize certain terminology to indicate the development of culture. The term *Paleolithic,* or Old Stone Age, for example, is the term which coincides in time with the geological epoch *Pleistocene.* Cultural periods within the Paleolithic are named for the stone industries which occurred or evolved within that larger block of time.

Divisions of the Paleolithic

The Paleolithic is divided into three segments: Lower (extending from the beginning of the Pleistocene to the third or Riss glaciation, a relatively long span of time); Middle (squeezed between the Riss and Würm glaciations); and Upper (beginning at the peak of the Würm glaciation and ending at the termination of the Pleistocene). In all, we are considering a time duration of nearly three million years.

We will now examine the development of culture from the Lower Paleolithic, considering the evolution of artifacts chronologically and geographically.

The Lower Paleolithic

A number of industries date from the Lower Paleolithic. Among them, according to geographical distribution, are the following:

EUROPE AND THE NEAR EAST

The earliest man-made tools to appear in Europe were found at a number of sites in present-day France and England.

1. *Abbevillian:* The earliest date appears to be late first interglacial. The *Abbevillian,* also known as *Chellean,* is a lithic industry characterized by large crude core tools that have been bifacially worked. These have been functionally classified as hand-axes or fist axes (see Figure 12).

A core tool is fashioned through the removal of flakes from a stone nodule until the desired shape has been achieved. Flake tools are made from the flakes previously removed from the core. In the former case, the basic core or nodule is used as a tool, while in the latter, the flake that has been removed is utilized. Early man used both types, although he often favored one or the other; that is, an industry may demonstrate a greater percentage of core tools than flake tools, or vice-versa.

A stone tool bifacially worked is one from which flakes were removed on both sides of the stone piece. Some weapons or tools are unifacially worked, i.e., prepared on only one side.

The Abbevillian lasted for a long time, from the first interglacial to the middle of the second interglacial. In other words, tools recognizable as Abbevillian have been found in sites that could be dated within this time period. The industry is limited to Europe, with most sites occurring along the Atlantic coast of France and Spain.

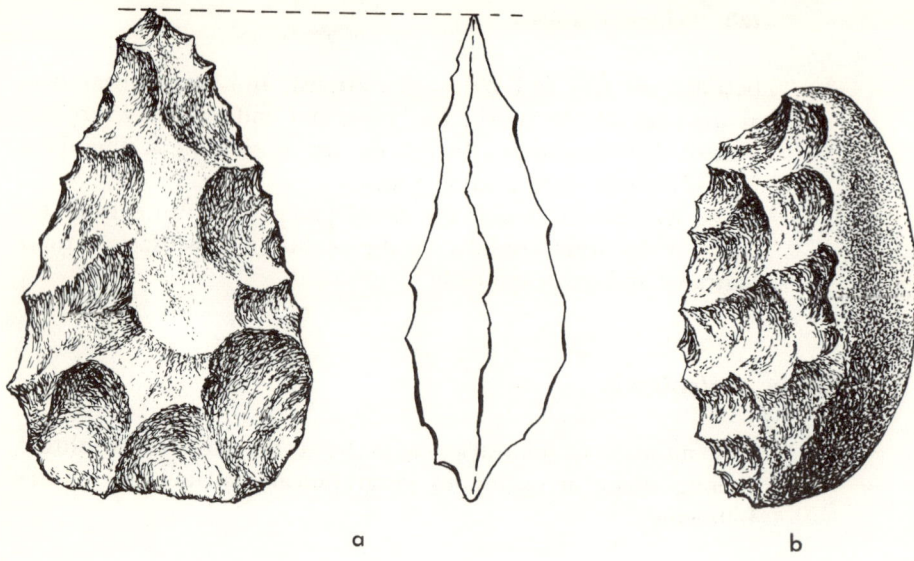

FIGURE 12 Typical tool types, Old World. (a) Handaxe; (b) chopper; (c) scraper; (d) tanged point; (e) blade; (f) burin.

Some flake tools are associated, but the typical Abbevillian specimen is a bifaced hand-ax, a core tool. Edges are not retouched, and length varies from three to six inches. So far, no human skeletal material has been found in association with the Abbevillian. The Heidelberg mandible, dated from this period, was not located in association with any artifacts.

2. *Clactonian:* The only other lithic industry dating from the same early time period as the Abbevillian is the Clactonian, originating from sites in England and elsewhere in Europe. The Clactonian occupies a time period from the first interglacial to the Riss glaciation.

Clactonian artifacts are not so distinctive as we would like; they are essentially large crude flakes that have been struck from a core which has been partially trimmed to help determine flake shape. These implements are primitive, and there seems to be little or no secondary retouching along the edges. Core tools are also present, in the form of unifacially worked tools called choppers (see Figure 12) in order to distinguish them from the bifacial hand-ax. Again, no human skeletal material has been associated to date.

3. *Acheulian:* An extension of the Abbevillian, the Acheulian begins in the middle of the second interglacial and ex-

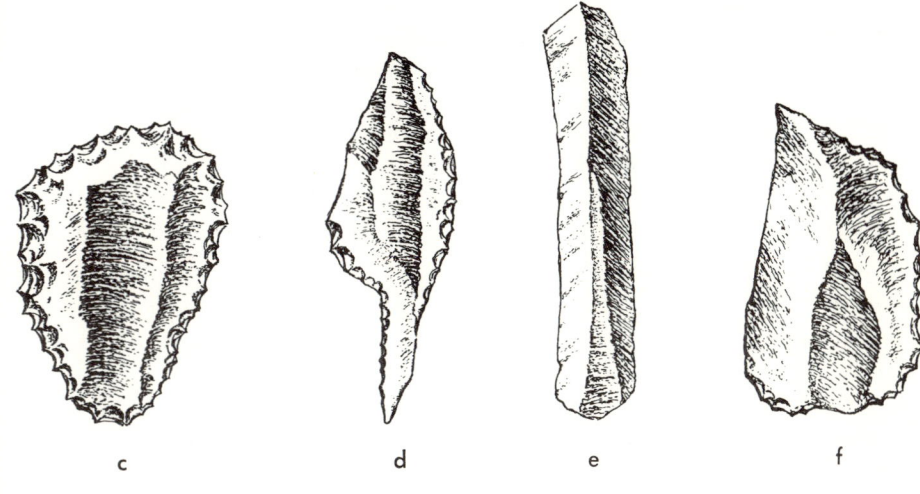

c　　　　　　　d　　　　　　e　　　　　　　f

tends into the middle Paleolithic. Bifaced hand-axes spread from the initial Abbevillian distribution in France and Spain to southern England, Italy, and in Europe to sites as far east as Palestine and Syria. The makers of these tools continued to favor core tools, but the Acheulian hand-axes tend to be flatter, more evenly flaked, and with more functional cutting edges. There is also a greater variety: the cleaver, also bifacially worked but having a wide cutting edge much like a modern butcher's cleaver rather than the pointed shape of the hand-ax, is introduced and spreads. All of this indicates a better control of the technique for making stone tools.

Human skeletal remains have been found in association with Acheulian: the fragmentary remains from Swanscombe. Because these remains are so scant, we haven't much of a picture of the people who were responsible for an industry so widespread as the Acheulian.

4. *Levalloisian:* Toward the end of the second interglacial, early man introduced a new method for producing flake tools. The Levalloisian is dated from the last third of the second interglacial and continues into the Middle Paleolithic. Actually, the Levalloisian represents an advanced technique of manufacturing flake tools by a special method of core preparation. By very

careful trimming, the core is shaped to resemble a tortoise shell. Small flakes are then removed from the perimeter of this tortoise core, and these flakes are reworked into a variety of scrapers and points. This technique, which probably represents early man's first attempt at mass production, spread throughout Europe, the Near East, southwest Asia, and Africa. Again the frustrating absence of human skeletal material leaves us in the dark concerning the people who invented this remarkable technique.

AFRICA

The earliest evidence of man-made tools occurs not in Europe, but in the dark continent. These tools are not much to look at, but they can reliably be distinguished from stones that have been naturally fractured. This crude assemblage is called the *Pre-Chelles-Acheul*.

1. *Pre-Chelles-Acheul:* Identified from sites in northwest, east, and south Africa, this industry is generally dated as pre-Mindel. The tools are roughly chipped from pebbles or cores taken from stream beds. There is no definite pattern, and they are sometimes accompanied by large, crude flakes.

There is still some doubt as to what early hominid was responsible for this industry. Associations have been demonstrated in east Africa (with remains of *Zinjanthropus boisei* and *Homo habilis*) and at some of the sites in south Africa (with remains of *Australopithecus*). Because of the tenuous nature of these associations, we are unable to make reliable conclusions concerning the actual manufacturers of the Pre-Chelles-Acheul tools. Also, at many of the south African sites, a bone tool industry, the *osteodontokeratic,* has been described by Dart [1] and associated with *Australopithecus africanus*. It is then possible that there are two types of tool industries in south Africa, each associated with different hominid populations. More evidence will eventually solve these problems.

2. *Chelles-Acheul:* Following the Pre-Chelles-Acheul and recognized as beginning with the earliest phases of the second interglacial, is the Chelles-Acheul. Here we find tools that look very much like the implements described in Europe. These large, bifaced hand-axes are found throughout Africa during the second interglacial and are eventually joined by cleavers.

---

[1] Dart, R. A. The Osteodontokeratic Culture of Australopithecus Prometheus. *Memoir, Transvaal Museum,* 10, Pretoria, 1957.

Through this whole period, large core tools prevail. It is not until the very end of the second interglacial that the Levalloisian technique is introduced and small flake tools become an important part of the African tool assemblages.

We do have some idea of the people who produced these tools. *Homo erectus* remains are found in east Africa (Chellean III) and northwest Africa at the Ternifine site *(Atlanthropus mauritanicus)*. Unfortunately, the skeletal evidence appears quite early in this period, and although the cultural evidence goes on to the end of the second interglacial, skeletal associations have not been found for the later phases.

ASIA

Geographically, Asia represents an area that begins in some parts of India and spreads throughout China, Malaysia, and the southeastern islands. Some authorities distinguish between a western and eastern tradition, and there seems to be evidence for this point of view. The *Pre-Soan* of India, the *Anyathian* of Burma, the *Choukoutienian* of China, and the *Patjitanian* of Java are characterized by what are often referred to as *chopper-chopping tools*. We have seen that choppers are unifacially worked tools; this style seems to be typical of the Asiatic stone industries. Core tools, chipped from one side and associated with crude flake tools (made from remnant flakes as by-products of the manufacture of choppers) are found in Asiatic sites throughout the second interglacial.

Excellent skeletal association occurs at Choukoutien, where a large sample of *Homo erectus (Sinanthropus)* has been found with good examples of these unifacial choppers (classified as *Choukoutienian*). As yet, this represents our only evidence of tools and man in Asia during the Lower Paleolithic.

The Middle Paleolithic

The people who lived in the Lower Paleolithic were not sedentary, but wandered from place to place in search of food sources. They camped on the edges of rivers or lakes but, as evidenced by the extremely thin deposits, did not remain very long in any single locale. There are no extensive refuse deposits and no burial areas, both indicators of human habitation of some duration. As we have seen, most of the evidence consists of the stone implements left behind on the erratic trails of nomadic restlessness.

In the Middle Paleolithic, however, the people settled down a bit. They demonstrated better techniques for making tools, and, toward the end of the third interglacial, many took advantage of cave living.

EUROPE AND THE NEAR EAST

There is a continuation of the industries described in the Lower Paleolithic. The Acheulian and the Levalloisian are found throughout the third interglacial. Changes in this tool assemblage do take place, but such changes generally represent no more than a sophistication of technique. Tools are smaller and more refined, with some special developments such as crude triangular points. There is no human skeletal material associated with these industries.

New industries appear for our inventory:

1. *Tayacian:* The Tayacian is a little known but important industry limited to a few scattered sites in France and Spain. Tools tend to be crude and simple, represented by rough flakes reminiscent of the earlier Clactonian. The importance of the Tayacian rests with its association with the fragmentary cranial remains from Fontechevade. The association as well as the early date for such modern skeletal material remains a puzzle for most experts.

2. *Mousterian:* The Mousterian is quite a different matter, for it is associated with *Homo neanderthalensis,* a population we are coming to know well through an excellent accumulation of skeletal evidence. Sites in Europe and the Near East are within rock shelters or caves. Tools include small heart-shaped hand-axes, triangular points, side scrapers and some simple bone awls (simple penetrating tools). It is interesting to note that in some European sites and especially in sites from Palestine, the Mousterian combines with the Levalloisian, characterized by the production of Mousterian-like tools made from Levalloisian flakes. The combination is complicated by the fact

that no human skeletal material has ever been associated with the Levalloisian.

Of course, the Neanderthals are responsible for the Mousterian or Levalloisio-Mousterian industry, and associations have been demonstrated during the third interglacial at Krapina, Saccopastore, Tabun, and Shanidar.

AFRICA

The third interglacial of most of Africa was warm and dry, and most sites are located along river banks and lake shores. The tool assemblages are similar to those in Europe, representing a continuation of the Chelles-Acheul and Levalloisian with certain local developments, two of which are worthy of special mention:

    1. *Sangoan:* Found in central, east, and south Africa, the Sangoan includes large crude hand-axes and slim picks, both bifacially worked. There are also large scrapers and triangular points, but the major phenomenon is a technique which produced elongated, bifacially flaked points or lance heads, not found in Europe or other areas of Africa.

    2. *Fouresmith:* Confined to East Africa and Rhodesia during this time period, the Fouresmith is found only in high altitudes, e.g., on Mt. Kilimanjaro and Mt. Kenya. There we find flat, ovate hand-axes, small triangular hand-axes, small cleavers, and numerous flake tools.

We have little knowledge of the people responsible for these stone industries. The Rhodesian skull has been placed in this time period, but due to the circumstances of its discovery, no reliable association can be made with the tools surrounding the area at Broken Hill.

ASIA

We are in a time period that has produced very little evidence concerning the tools manufactured or the people who made them. We can only assume that people did live in Asia and that they still fashioned tools of stone with which to cope with the daily problems of feeding themselves and defending themselves from carnivorous invasions, or—quite possibly—from representatives of their own kind.

The Upper Paleolithic

Following the first maximum of the Würm glaciation in Europe, as well as the rest of the Old World, a radical change in stone tools took place. During this period, man made his greatest cultural progress. Also, the Upper Paleolithic is ushered in by the replacement of Neanderthal man by Homo sapiens, who still made and used stone tools but with a new and different emphasis.

Blades (long, narrow flakes struck from cores), burins (chisels produced by striking small spawls at forty-five degree angles from the end of a flake or blade) and bone tools reached a maximum of production toward the end of the Upper Paleolithic (see Figure 12). Also, the remnant evidence of dwellings begin to appear. Semi-subterranean pit houses had been used in central Europe, Southern Russia, and Siberia. These living accomodations suggest a more complex social life and represent a completely new way of life for a people that looked very much like us.

Names and classifications of the variety of industries become somewhat confusing, due not only to the general variability of these industries but also to the great amount of local differentiation. Compared with what we have seen in earlier times, where basic cultural similarities are the rule, it is interesting to note the great diversification that is typical of the closing phases of the Paleolithic.

EUROPE AND THE NEAR EAST

The single holdover from the Middle Paleolithic is the Mousterian. It is characterized by better technical development and several local industries. The essential tools include triangular points, side scrapers and other types of flake tools, small handaxes, some simple bone tools, and—for the first time—rare blades and burins.

The disappearance of the Neanderthals and their culture occurred sometime during the first interstadial of the Würm glaciation. No one knows what happened, and the only evidence we have is negative. Neanderthal burials, so prevalent before, are no longer found. Certain elements of the Mousterian industry did continue in later Upper Paleolithic industries, but the true Mousterian ceased to exist with the disappearance of its founders, another mystery in the development of mankind that we leave to the imagination and efforts of future archeologists and paleoanthropologists.

1. *Perigordian:* The earliest Upper Paleolithic industry associated with the appearance of sapiens populations is the Perigordian. It has been recognized in sites dating from the first interstadial, contemporary with the Mousterian, and continues to the peak of the third advance of the Würm glaciation. The early tool assemblage is essentially limited to southern France and includes large blades, burins, scrapers, and some simple bone tools. Similar tool types have been found in Palestine, and there are some who believe that the origin of the European Perigordian—as well as the people who produced it —should be placed somewhere in the Middle East.

As we follow the development of the Perigordian into the later phases of the Upper Paleolithic, some dynamic changes in the basic tool types are apparent. First, the industry spread from its initial beginnings in France to a general European distribution. The large blades give way to small, narrow backed blades and a variety of specialized burins. Also, we find tanged points (stemmed) that have been manufactured from blades.

The people responsible for the Perigordian were found at a number of sites and are classified as Cro Magnon (*Homo sapiens sapiens*).

2. *Aurignacian:* Dating from Würm II to the middle of Würm III, the Aurignacian is found at many sites between the earliest and most recent phases of the Perigordian. Also, there is a similar geographic distribution, from France to Palestine and Syria. The tool types are in some cases indistinguishable, with many types of scrapers, blades, and burins. However, the one feature that differentiates the Aurignacian from the Perigordian is the use of bone in the former. The most typical are crude bone points with split bases. Also, bone needles and articles are personal adornment (necklaces of pierced teeth and shells decorated with bits of bone) are an important element of the Aurignacian assemblage.

Art, as we know it, made its first appearance in the Aurignacian of Europe. However crude, art in its earliest manifestation is impressive. Profile drawings of various animals on cave walls in black and red and pointed hands represent the early artistic efforts of Paleolithic man.

The Aurignacian is associated with the human skeletal material from Grimaldi.

3. *Solutrean:* One of the more mysterious industries—and one of the most aesthetic—of the European Upper Paleolithic is the Solutrean (see Figure 13). It lasted a very short period of time, ranging around the maximum of the third advance of the Würm glaciation. Sites have been found in France, Hungary, Poland, Spain, and southern Russia. The founders of the Solutrean are noted for having produced the finest example of stone workmanship. The technique of parallel flaking on both faces produced beautiful, symmetrical laurel-leaf blades and shouldered points. These very specialized tools are unique to the Solutrean and are not found anywhere else in the world. Except for the distinctive laurel-leaf blades and shouldered points noted above, the remainder of Solutrean tool types are indistinguishable from the Perigordian.

Of course, we would like to know the people who manufactured these remarkable implements, but, unfortunately, no human skeletal material has ever been found at any Solutrean site. Predmost, Brunn, and La Roc skeletal material is usually assigned to the Solutrean cultural period, but no clear association between human remains and Solutrean artifacts has yet been seen.

4. *Magdalenian:* Extending from Würm III to the end of the Pleistocene, the Magdalenian represents the last of the European Upper Paleolithic industries. During this time, the climate was extremely cold; the most abundant animal living then was the reindeer. The Magdalenian is strictly European in distribution, with sites located in England, Germany, France, Spain, and Italy.

The outstanding trend during the Magdalenian is the decline of stone tools and their replacement with a variety of bone tools. The basic tool form was a harpoon point (see Figure 13). In fact, some authorities have divided the Magdalenian into six developmental stages based on the evolution of the harpoon point. Also, the art which had begun during the Aurignacian reached a peak during the Magdalenian. The early crude profiles gave way to distinctive three-dimensional polychrome represen-

FIGURE 13 Upper Paleolithic tool types, Old World. (a) Solutrean point; (b) Magdalenian harpoon (bone).

tations of the various animals that these people hunted. The caves of Lascaux in southern France and Altimira in northern Spain demonstrate the unique nature of the artistic excellence during the Upper Paleolithic.

The Magdalenian industry, with its bone tools and art, cannot be duplicated anywhere else in the world. It is associated with the skeletal remains from Chancelade and Obercassel, which some experts have classified as Mongoloid. Mongoloid physical features and tools reminiscent of modern Eskimo cultures lead some people to hypothesize on the origin of recent circumpolar populations. As yet, this is only an interesting speculation.

AFRICA

During the Upper Paleolithic, African industries began to deviate from the amazing unanimity that prevailed through most of the Paleolithic. The tool assemblages found at the end of this period demonstrate remarkable variation.

In north Africa, two industries dominated the Upper Paleolithic:

1. *Aterian:* Found in sites from Morocco to Egypt, the Aterian was first thought to be Mousterian, but later was recognized as a variation of what we know as the Levalloisio-Mousterian. Typical tools include tanged points and spear blades up to nine inches in length. Origin of the Aterian is probably to the south and some experts see associations with the Sangoan. As yet, there are no positive human skeletal associations.

2. *Capsian:* Found in Algeria and superficially reminiscent of European industries, the Capsian tools are extremely small (microlithic). Small blades and burins were probably, because of their size, fitted into slots on bone or wooden handles. They were certainly too small to be functionally used in the hand. Skeletal associations point to early *Homo sapiens sapiens* populations.

In north Africa, Egypt seems to represent an isolated cultural development:

3. *Sebilian:* This industry obviously has its roots in the African Levalloisian, but the stone tools made from Levallois flakes become smaller and smaller until they can be classified as microlithic. So, rather than producing new tool types, the Sebilian is simply a microlithic Levalloisian and seems to be unknown in other areas of Africa. No human skeletal material is associated.

In east Africa, the Capsian prevails in a number of sites, but there is also a continuation of the Levalloisian called Stillbay.

4. *Stillbay:* Characterized by triangular points with bifacial retouching but produced from Levalloisian flakes, the Stillbay is distinguished from earlier Levalloisian in the great variation of tool types produced from flakes struck from tortoise cores. Again, no human skeletal material is associated.

In south Africa, the Fouresmith continues with its small handaxes and unifacial Levalloisian flake tools. As yet the Capsian, or the general microlithic trend to the north, has not been found in this area. The Stillbay, in most sites, continues to the end of the Paleolithic. Human skeletal remains are absent.

ASIA

We know very little about the late cultural manifestations of Asia. Insufficient investigation has been accomplished, and only one industry has been well described.

1. *Ordosian:* Occurring in northern China, the Ordosian is a little known assemblage partially reminiscent of the western Mousterian, yet the inventory includes burins and micro-blades along with typical points and scrapers. The date is fourth glacial, or a time equivalent to the European fourth glacial, and we are told that the people responsible for the Ordosian are Neanderthal. Certainly Asia has much to add to our knowledge of Paleolithic prehistory. We can only wait and see.

A survey of the tools throughout the Paleolithic of the Old World forces us to conclude that the people who lived during this time were dependent on a hunting-fishing-gathering economy. There was no horticulture or agriculture. As for domestication of animals, there is some evidence that the dog may have been domesticated in the late Paleolithic of Europe. In post-Pleistocene times, changes in the ecological conditions were so great and so relatively sudden that they gave rise to major readjustments in the sphere of culture.

True domestication of plants and animals began in the Mesolithic (the cultural period following the Paleolithic) somewhere in western Asia. This process led in the course of a few centuries to the rise of economies in which hunting and fishing became subsidiary to that of agriculture and stock-raising. It was the practice of both that provided a firm basis for the earliest civilizations of the Old World.

The New World

We have been fortunate in accumulating for the Old World a relatively stable framework in which we can define cultural developments, however fragmentary our knowledge may be at present. For the New World, of course, since man arrived there late and equipped with material culture, our developmental sequence begins not with the crude, primitive tools we saw in the Old World but with a number of evolved tool complexes.

In the New World, we are particularly dependent upon the cultural remains left behind, for we have scant evidence to reflect the physical remains of these people.

Human occupation of parts of North and South America has been conclusively demonstrated for as early as thirteen thousand years ago, but it is fairly certain that man was in the New World by at least thirty to forty thousand years ago, probably arriving by way of a land or ice bridge across the Bering Straits between northeast Asia and Alaska. So, following our coverage of the Old World, we will consider only the evidence in the New World that can be attributed to the Pleistocene.

From the archeological evidence that we have, it is clear that we are dealing with a single cultural way of life: big game hunting. There is little or no indication of increased population density or of a shift to a more sedentary settlement pattern.

The earliest culture is designated as Paleo-Indian. Two distinct types of projectile points—Sandia and Clovis—compete as evidence for the earliest remains of man in North America. Although they have never been found in the same site, most experts feel that Sandia is earlier on a typological basis (the technique of making such a point).

SANDIA

The Sandia projectile point is restricted in its geographical distribution to the west and southwest of north America. It is characterized (see Figure 14) by a stem or tang on one side at the base of the point. It has been found with fluting (a groove running down the middle of the face of the point) or with partial fluting associated with a concave base.

CLOVIS

This point (see Figure 14) has a wide geographical distribution, being found in Alaska, Canada, and at a number of sites in north, central, and south America. It has always been found at the lowest level in the site and usually associated with the butchered remains of mammoths. Carbon-14 dates suggest eleven to thirteen thousand years; the probable closing date for this projectile point is nine thousand years.

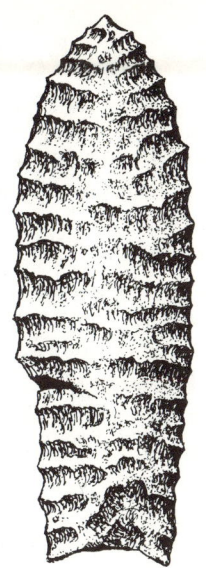
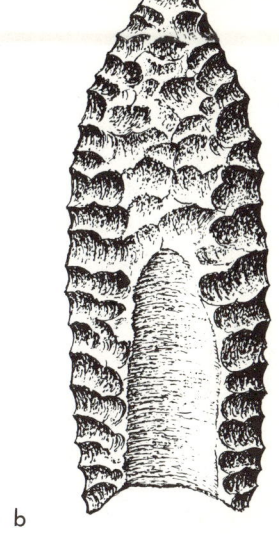

FIGURE 14 Typical projectile points, New World. (a) Sandia; (b) Clovis; (c) Folsom; (d) lanceolate type.

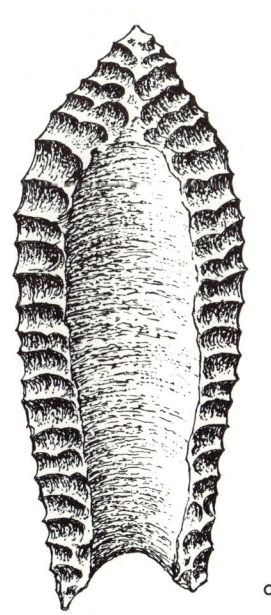
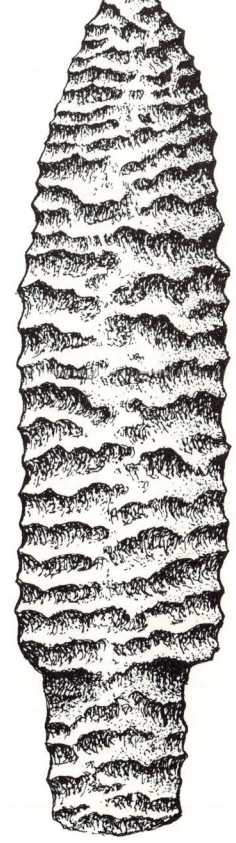

121

FOLSOM

Our next clue to the cultural propensities of early man in the New World is represented by another projectile point designated as Folsom (see Figure 14).

The Folsom point also has a wide distribution but has been found mostly west of the Mississippi, where it is located stratigraphically above (or more recent than) the Clovis points. It is interesting that the dominant animal associated with Folsom points is not mammoth but bison. Carbon-14 dates place the Folsom culture between nine and ten thousand years ago.

The Folsom point is fluted, sometimes bifacially, and demonstrates parallel flaking at some of the sites.

The Folsom ends the Paleo-Indian tradition and ushers in a variety of apparently related lanceolate projectile points (see Figure 14). The main characteristic is the technique of parallel flaking, which represents the acme of flint workmanship in the New World. This tradition ends with the onset of altithermal climate (the period of maximum dryness and warmth in Post-Pleistocene times). This period witnessed the extinction of the last of the great Pleistocene big-game animals.

This is certainly a very brief summary of human activities during the late phases of the Pleistocene of the New World. However, that is all the evidence we have. Other than these well-made projectile points, our knowledge of the early populations of the New World rests with a number of doubtful examples of the skeletal remains of these early voyagers. Let us consider two of the best documented representatives.

TEPEXPAN

In 1947, this site in Mexico produced the remains of a male skeleton about fifty years old, associated with the bones of a mammoth and flake tools made of obsidian. The morphology of the skeleton is not remarkable; in fact, it resembles the modern population of central Mexico. However, a Carbon-14 date places the Tepexpan skeleton at about eleven thousand years ago.

MIDLAND

From this site in Texas we have the partial human skeleton of a thirty-year-old female with a long, narrow skull. The human remains are associated with stone tools (Folsom) and extinct animal bones. A fluorine analysis substantiates its placement in the site, and Carbon-14 dates indicate an age of about nine thousand years.

This brief sample of the early populations known to have invaded the north American continent in late Pleistocene times is anything but impressive. We should mention that there is quite a list of early skeletal finds from both north and south America, but in each case the evidence is suspect. Compared to the Old World, the New World story, at least what we know of it, is rather disappointing. However, the mystery of exactly who made their way into the New World, and when, remains an intriguing question and should stimulate future students in an area of investigation that represents one of the fundamental problems of man's development in this hemisphere.

Suggested Readings

Clark, J. D.
    1963. The evolution of culture in Africa. *Amer. Nat.* 97:15–28.

Clark, Grahame
    1962. *World Prehistory, An Outline.* Cambridge: University of Cambridge Press.

Gabel, Creighten (ed.)
    1964. *Man Before History.* Englewood Cliffs, N.J.: Prentice-Hall, Inc.

Hole, Frank, and Robert F. Heizer
    1965. *An Introduction to Prehistoric Archeology.* New York: Holt, Rinehart & Winston.

Krieger, Alex D.
    1964. Early man in the new world. *In:* Jesse D. Jennings and Edward Norbeck (eds.) *Prehistoric Man in the New World.* Chicago: University of Chicago Press.

PRIMATOLOGY

chapter
9

If we are to study anthropology in the truest sense of the word—that is, to strive toward full understanding of man—our knowledge of the human organism should extend down to its lower primate origins. By knowing every possible aspect of man's closest relatives, we approach a solution to some of the basic problems of human evolution.

Methods of Investigation

Research in *primatology*—the study of the living primates from both the biological and the social viewpoints—can be conducted in three ways: the animals involved may be studied within their natural environment, in artificially established colonies such as those seen in zoos, or in the laboratory. Each approach has inherent advantages and disadvantages, but all contribute to the accumulation of knowledge of man's relatives and, by inference, of man's early life.

Observation of the group in the field has the advantage of preserving as fully as possible normal patterns of behavior. It may be argued that the very presence of the observer constitutes a disruptive influence and therefore induces abnormal behavior in the groups under study. Trained observers, however, take great pains to minimize the effect of their presence. In most cases, the investigator incorporates into his field schedule a period of time at the outset, during which he attempts to establish a neutral relationship with the group. He seeks from the animals neither approval (by hope for reward) or disapproval (by fear of punishment or pain). Most observers have found that following a relatively brief period of adjustment, the primate group will revert to normal behavior, tolerating (or, in many cases, simply ignoring) the investigator. At this time, the normal behavior of the animals under study may be observed and recorded. Later, the investigator may wish to inject a deliberately disruptive factor in order to observe reactions to new or unfamiliar situations.

There are other limitations on the use of field studies. The natural habitat of a particular group of animals may be inaccessible to human investigators. Further, in order to obtain the most reliable results, field studies should be of lengthy duration, taking into account seasonal or cyclic patterns of behavior. Yet climatic factors or geographical limitations may preclude a prolonged study.

In many cases, however, the field study is crucial when other methods of investigation cannot be used. The baboon, for example, is unsuitable for colony and most laboratory studies, due primarily to its size and temperament. In such cases, we are forced to rely upon data obtained through field observation (see Figure 15).

The use of information gleaned from observation in artificially established colonies is restricted by its very nature. The scientist cannot be certain that behavior noted under artificial circumstances is valid or typical of group life in the wild. Moreover, some groups are unsuitable for colonization. Again the baboon provides an example. In 1925, *S. Zuckerman* directed the establishment of a baboon colony at the Regent's Park Zoo in London, beginning with a group of one hundred individuals, predominantly male. Within two years, only fifty-six were left, the rest dying in sexual battles. Hoping to better match the sexes and reduce combat, the Zoo brought in an additional

FIGURE 15 For measurement, actual capture must be effected. These caged specimens await field mensuration. Measurements are made by the quickest means possible; when measurements are complete, baboons are released in natural habitat. *Photo courtesy of William R. Maples.*

thirty-five colony members—thirty females and five immature males; within sixty days, fifteen females were killed. By 1930, only thirty-nine males and nine females were left, the females "owned" by the eight dominant males of the group. Out of fifteen baboons born during the duration of the colony, only one survived (the others accidentally were squeezed to death during sexual battles). Before dismissing the baboon as a uniquely unsavory character, however, we might note that self-destruction is hardly limited to baboon society. Those familiar with *Mutiny on the Bounty* will recall that fifteen males (nine English, six Tahitian) were left on Pitcairn Island with twelve females. Ten years later, though the females fared well enough, only one male survived. This suggests that the baboon might have illustrious company in its unsuitability for laboratory study.

Laboratory studies—for those groups of animals that are suitable—have the distinct advantage of permitting mental and psychological testing. While such investigation tends to shed little light on group behavior in the appropriate natural habitat, it yields excellent data on intelligence and memory. Scientists have devised numerous tests to gauge in nonhuman primates the use of past experience and concept of future, means of intercommunication, and tool use; these are but representative of the many fields open to inquiry in the laboratory. For an example of a typical test, we can refer to the classic "Chimp-O-Mat" experiment conducted by *W. Kohler* in the 1920's in order to gauge past experience and concept of future. In this test, Kohler used a vending machine filled with raisins; the chimpanzee under observation was forced to work for tokens (poker chips), after which he could use his earned tokens to buy raisins from the machine. The chimpanzee complied with relative ease. Later, the machine was purposely put out of order. The chimpanzee continued to work for tokens, saving them in apparent anticipation of a buying spree once the machine resumed work.

Kohler concluded that neither memory—that is, the use of past experience—nor concept of future was utilized by the chimpanzee. The familiar situation appeared under the same psychological conditions that existed during his learning period, bringing about the same choice of behavior. In simpler terms, the chimp's behavior was governed by the predictable results of conditioned response. Further, said Kohler, the behavior that solves the problem arises from a consideration of the *present* rather than of the future. Animals are carried away by their immediate and narrow interest in the goal before them—food.

While Kohler's conclusions have been challenged—perhaps validly—his methods serve to illustrate the type of testing conducted in modern laboratories. And the fact that his views have been attacked points to another limitation on laboratory study of primates: the human factor. Whatever testing is done can be only as reliable as the human analysis of the test results.

Of course, not all primates are suitable for laboratory study. The orangutan, for example, seems to be innately lazy. One investigator worked with a single orang for twenty-three consecutive days without eliciting response, then was amazed to see him solve a series of problems in a matter of seconds. The baboon, as we have seen, is unsuitable because of temperament; his behavior is too unpredictable for laboratory testing and he must be handled with caution. The gorilla is difficult to work with and can be dangerous; he can be cunning and crafty but may brood and rebel. Despite these limitations, his memory is excellent: one specimen, after ten months, resumed a previous experiment without apparent hesitation.

Of all the nonhuman primates, the chimpanzee is best suited for laboratory analysis. He is the extrovert of the group, cooperative and eager, and seems always to enjoy the experiments. The chimp performs best in problem-solving tests. He manifests behavior of the general kind familiar to human beings. For this reason, the chimpanzee stands out above the rest of the animal kingdom and exhibits a type of behavior that is distinctively human.

Ideally, each group of primates should be studied from each of the three basic approaches. This is seldom feasible, though scientists continue to strive toward the fullest possible data, gleaned from every available source.

Perhaps most relevant to our purposes is that information demonstrating social organization among each group of nonhuman primates. From this knowledge come our hypotheses regarding the early social life of man. It might be helpful at this point to review our accumulated knowledge of representative primates from studies in the field and in the laboratory.

The Howler Monkey

The classic study of the howler monkey, selected here to represent an example of our knowledge of the Ceboidea, was completed in 1934 by *C. R. Carpenter;* numerous studies since that time have examined the habits of this group. The howler (*Alouatta palliata*), ranging from Mexico to the forests of Central and South America, features the expected three premolar teeth and prehensile tail, which is used as an additional hand.

The howler prefers never to leave the trees; when forced to walk, however, it uses all four limbs—of which the great toe is opposable while the thumb is not—and can swim, though reluctantly. Most movement is confined to the upper reaches of the forest, however, and is conducted with the body in pronograde position. Locomotion is slow and deliberate except in moods of excitation; leaping from branch to branch is rare. Contact is maintained through the prehensile tail when spaces between branches on trees are bridged.

The howler receives its name from its peculiar means of communication, a high-pitched scream or wail. This vocationalization is made morphologically possible by an inflation of the hyoid bone in the throat. In man, the hyoid is slender and horseshoe-shaped; in the howler, it is expanded into a large bubble of bone, through which sound is vibrated and magnified. Anyone who has traveled through the forest regions of South America recalls with amazement the cry of the howler monkey.

The howler feeds directly from the tree branches, seldom holding food in its hands. Much food is wasted, as howlers drop a large proportion of what they pick; this is due apparently to the limited manipulation afforded by the hand. Food includes fruits, nuts, and leaves. Water is obtained primarily through food content, and howlers rarely leave the trees to drink from streams. After a heavy rain, they may lick moisture from leaves or collect it on their hands, licking it from the skin and hair.

Howlers group in clans of two to forty-five individuals. Each clan occupies a well defined territory—including particular food or lodging trees and pathways between—seldom exceeding three hundred acres. Clan members do not venture outside the boundaries of their chosen territory. Travel is limited and erratic. Adult males generally lead a march, though no definite leadership has been observed.

No dominance pattern is apparent. There are usually more females than males, and these—particularly during *estrus* (the height of sexual receptivity)—become aggressive and promiscuous, mating indiscriminately among available males. There appears to be no jealously or competition among the males for the clan females. Apparently, the females control.

Social control is accomplished through noise—howling. There are frequent howling battles between clans, usually to protect clan members or defend their territory. The clan itself lacks the degree of closure prevalent among primate groups. While a group may tend to remain together as a whole, it may on occasion divide or split, or individual members—generally complementary males—may leave to join a new group. This is accomplished by following closely, making repeated attempts to approach, and finally absorbing into the group. A male who has left for a period of time may return to his original group. He may or may not be accepted.

As will be obvious in the coming pages, the howler group exhibits a loose social organization relative to that characteristic of the higher primates.

The Baboon

The earliest field studies of the baboon were undertaken by S. *Zuckerman* at Cape Province, South Africa, in 1932. Zuckerman's choice for study was the chacma baboon. His research in the field was limited by the brevity of time allocated for field study, but he recorded data later affirmed by more comprehensive investigations. Most of our information for the baboon has been gathered in the field, due to the animal's unsuitability for laboratory analysis.

The baboon (*Papio*) exhibits the expected characteristics of a Cercopithecoid. Its dental formula is 2:1:2:3. It features both cheek pouches and ischial callosities (callouses on the buttocks). The baboon is, however, atypical in that it is a terrestrial animal and exhibits numerous adaptations to a terrestrial habitat: the elongated snout, tusk-like canines, and arms and legs of equal length. In the female the sexual skin around the callosities swells during estrus to enormous proportions and is often brilliantly hued.

The baboon is found in Africa south of the Sahara Desert and in the peninsula region of Arabia. A diurnal animal, it feeds during the daylight hours and climbs into the trees at night to rest. Baboons group and travel in groups of between thirty and one hundred individuals. Each troop requires a large territorial range in order to derive ultimate benefit from natural resources; the baboon is chiefly vegetarian. Despite this fact, he is classed as omnivorous, for most baboons supplement their vegetarian diet with insects, lizards, birds, and eggs. They may also attack and kill small animals for food and have been known to kill and disembowel lambs for the curdled milk in their stomachs.

Contact between different troops is limited. Within the group, behavior is stabilized through the existence and enforcement of a social hierarchy in which males dominate. Frequently, there is a single male leader—usually the most aggressive and physically fit—and codominants of lesser rank. These lesser-ranked males dominate over other males and females in the troop.

The leader baboon is fiercely protective, particularly of the mothers and young of the troop. When danger is apparent (see Figure 16), he is the first to advance. Competition for the leadership role seems rigorous, and the tenure of the chief baboon is seldom long. He leads only until challenged and defeated by another male, his most likely successors coming from the ranks of the bachelor males. These watch closely until they sense a weakening in their leader, then move rapidly to take over his females, and subsequently his command, whenever that weakening occurs. Bachelor males who do not assume power remain unmated throughout their lives; they are usually heterosexual and assume low-ranking positions in the troop.

Family organization is centered, predictably, around the male overlord and his chosen females; added to this group are the young and the unmated bachelor males. There seems always to be a favorite female: she is the one currently mating with the leader, staying close to his side and grooming him frequently. In return, she is rewarded with some of his food and the status of harem leader, dominating over the lesser females. The females are consistently submissive and rarely unfaithful, but they change loyalties rapidly to adjust to the appearance of new leaders.

Zuckerman and others have noted in troop movements a complete defense position assumed by troop members. Females and youngsters are guarded in the center by males in front, at the rear, and in flank position. Solitary baboons are almost never seen; the dangers encountered in man and leopard are

FIGURE 16   Angry male baboon shown with fangs bared.
Photo courtesy of William R. Maples.

so feared that movement is confined to the troop. When an individual is forced to retire for a time from the group, as in the case of accident or illness, he seeks sanctuary above ground levels and returns to the group as soon as possible. And while a lone baboon will seldom challenge an enemy, the group will and often does. Because each female may give birth annually, troops continue to grow in size, unchecked by any epidemic which would naturally limit population. Emboldened by sheer numbers, the larger troops may pillage orchards and fields and pose a threat to sheep and other small livestock. The problem has become so extreme in many areas that bounties are offered for baboon destruction.

Viewed relative to the representative Ceboidea, the baboon

group demonstrates a higher degree of social organization. This is illustrated by the solidarity of the troop—from which members seldom stray—and in the obvious social hierarchy which controls behavior of individual baboons.

The Gibbon

C. R. Carpenter also investigated, in 1940, the gibbon of southeast Asia. The gibbon (*Hylobates*) is a slender, agile pongid, morphologically adapted to locomotion by brachiation. Its arms are long, as are its hands and fingers. Movement through the trees is extremely efficient—the gibbon is the best brachiator known—but bipedalism is an awkward feat, accomplished with much swinging of the extended arms and tottering constantly in an obvious struggle for balance.

Perhaps ninety per cent of gibbon locomotion is by means of brachiation; therefore, the typical posture is orthograde, the spinal column held in an almost perpendicular plane. Fully at home in the trees, the gibbon may jump from twelve to fifteen feet, seldom with hesitation. Visual acuity is excellent; nearsighted gibbons simply do not survive. In the trees, sight is of crucial value; misjudgment results in a plunge to the ground below.

The gibbon is quite fussy about what he eats, limiting himself primarily to fruit—often bitter or sour—and leaves, although some insects are eaten. Feeding is done in a leisurely one-armed manner. Less hurried than its primate relatives, the gibbon neither robs nor drops, but carefully selects the food needed and feeds comfortably while hanging from a single arm. Water is obtained from dew fall or rain on leaves and body hair; the gibbon seldom ventures to a stream, as it finds walking awkward and is completely helpless in water.

Carpenter noted among his observed groups a well regulated daily schedule. The gibbon day begins early, at about 5:30 A.M., and ends by 6:00 P.M. In between, the gibbon feeds, grooms, and indulges in a noon siesta. Alone among the pongidae, the gibbon does not construct nests, but settles into a tree crotch for napping and nocturnal sleeping. Travel is not extensive, averaging perhaps eighteen hundred to two thousand yards a day, almost always in the upper reaches of trees.

The basic social unit is the primary family—an adult male, a female, and their progeny. More than one adult male or female is never found in a single unit. Competition incites animosity, precluding such a multiple arrangement. Those gibbons too aged to be useful or to keep pace with their families lead a solitary existence, as do those in a transition stage of breaking from their parental unit. Mating is largely monogamous.

The gibbon has a low sexual drive and no particular breeding season or estrus. Reproduction, however, is effective. Life span ranges between thirty and forty years, and the female gibbon is sexually active for at least twenty years of her life.

Family ties are close, and the relationship between mother and young is one of dependence. The female characteristically carries her young low on her pelvis, toward the front of her body, where it is protected from harm or injury. In time, the female pushes her infant out on its own, to join other unattached delinquents.

Grooming takes up most of the waking hours not devoted to feeding. Most primates groom because they like the salty taste of scales found around the pores of the skin. For the partner, the process eliminates the need to scratch. Groom is reciprocal: a gibbon who grooms another expects a prompt return of that favor. There is evidence also that the grooming function serves to express affection; whether this idea is valid or not, grooming appears to be a pleasurable experience for each partner.

The gibbon is highly territorial, and while his territory constantly shifts with migration, the gibbon will fiercely defend it as it is bounded at the time of threat. Gibbons prefer bluffing to fighting, and they will attempt to drive off an enemy with extended screeching and hooting. When a bluff fails, the gibbon resorts to physical combat, using his long sharp canines as highly effective weapons.

Sexual dominance is strangely absent among the gibbons, seemingly distributed equally among males and females. This lack of obvious dominance is most probably related to the general lack of sexual dimorphism among the gibbons. In other words, males and females are basically similar in size, strength, and appearance. When the sexes blur, apparently even the gibbons are not able to delegate authority.

The Orangutan

The orangutan (*Pongo*) is one of the few primates who adapt quite successfully to artificially established colonies. Confined naturally to Borneo and Sumatra, they appear quite happy in captivity, and some experts estimate that perhaps half of the total orang population is now housed in the various zoos of the world.

The orang is strictly vegetarian in diet, feeding off the natural resources without reliance on supplementary insects or small reptiles. Water is obtained through food content and from dew fall.

Of all the primates, the orang seems most closely related to the gibbon, and it is often suggested that the two should not be placed in separate families or subfamilies. Certainly the two are morphologically similar, featuring in particular the same long arms.

The orang lives in small family groups. Although little data is available on social organization, it is apparently the primary family that provides the basic social unit. The orang is typically gentle and quiet, with aggressiveness at a minimum among groups. Despite his rather ragged appearance, he is among the most popular zoo animals.

The Gorilla

The gorilla (*Gorilla*) is presently divided into two groups, the mountain and the lowland gorilla, but is believed to have once existed as a continuous population. Numerous studies have been completed on the gorilla in the field, perhaps the most extensive to date being that published in 1963 by George Schaller, describing his lengthy field observations of the mountain groups.

The gorilla is too large and heavy to be successfully arboreal and so is primarily terrestrial. Posture is frequently vertical—

in feeding, grooming, and playing—but bipedalism is rare and awkward. As a rule, locomotion is accomplished by use of the forelimbs, knuckles turned under, in a loping quadrupedal gait. Walking upright is restricted to short distances. Despite the limitations of size, the gorilla ascends into the trees to nest. Lodging nests are clumsily and hastily constructed of materials at hand.

Feeding is begun immediately after awakening. The gorilla is vegetarian and consumes immense amounts of food, generally staying on a single position and pulling from arm's reach all the available vegetation. After two or three hours of steady feeding, the gorilla rests, usually in a ground nest. Feeding is resumed after noon and continues, with interruptions for play and grooming, until late afternoon, when the gorilla returns to the nest (or constructs a new one) for sleeping.

Gorillas live in groups of between two and thirty individuals, although lone males are noted. These may continue to be solitary or rejoin one group or another seemingly at will. Lone females have not been observed. Aggressiveness between groups is not acute; apparently, neighboring groups have repeated and tolerant contacts with one another.

Size dominates, and the leader of each troop is generally the largest silver-backed male; the silver mane comes with age. Lesser males dominate in a linear hierarchy. Grooming among adult males is rare but occurs frequently among females and juveniles.

The dependence relationship between mother and young is lengthy, often lasting three years. Females give birth in not less than three or four years after the previous gestation.

Estrus among female gorillas is difficult to discern in the field, but zoo surveys have revealed the probability of a monthly cycle, with three to four days of heightened receptivity. The monthly cycle precludes a set breeding season, and Schaller's birthdate figures conform. Gestation ranges from 250 to 300 days.

Despite myth, gorillas tend to be placid, nonaggressive, and restrained in social temperament. They lead a quiet life, feeding and playing among themselves so long as they are not threatened. Since few carnivores inhabit their territory, they are not often the target of attack, and their primary enemy is man himself. In the face of danger, the gorilla prefers to bluff, standing erect and posturing wildly, beating his chest and charging for short distances. Forced to physical combat, the battle pattern is bite-and-retreat.

The Chimpanzee

The chimpanzee (*Pan*) is perhaps the most familiar of all the primates because of its popularity in circuses, zoos, and laboratories. The chimp, uniquely adaptable, submits as willingly to space research and laboratory testing as to human dress and lessons in bicycle-riding or skating. In the laboratory, he is cooperative, eager to please, and curious, making him an excellent subject for experimentation, particularly in the psychological or mental testing areas.

Numerous excellent studies have been compiled for the chimpanzee. Of these, perhaps the best known are those growing out of the Yerkes primate laboratory center, notably by Nissen. The Reynolds and Reynolds study of chimps in the Budongo Forest region of Africa, as well as the exciting reports from Jane Goodall on her work in the Gombe Stream Reserve, are examples of the meticulous attention to detail and devotion to accuracy characteristic of the leading field workers. These are the studies which will enable us to know better and better this primate that so often mirrors human behavior.

Confined naturally to Africa, two major species of chimpanzee have been noted: *Pan satyrus,* enjoying a wide distribution in equatorial Africa, and *Pan paniscus,* the pygmy chimp centered in a small area south of the Congo River. Of these, the former is the best known.

Perhaps the most distinct observation of chimpanzee life that has been noted is the loose social structure of chimp groups in the wild. Unlike the baboons, which exhibit a linear social organization inherent in a group of any size, the basic social unit for the chimpanzee consists of a temporary association of individuals for varying lengths of time. The only stable group observed is that of the mother/infant. These are joined periodically by other males and females of differing ages. Mature chimps, both male and female, are seen alone, an observation unparalleled among other pongids.

Presumably because of this fluid social grouping, patterns of dominance are indistinct. Aggressive-submissive relationships are infrequent. There is no clear leader; any chimp that initiates group movement or regulates its route or speed assumes—for the duration only—leadership status. But in this case rank carries no particular privilege. In individual interaction, observers have noted that mature males dominate over females and juveniles, while mature females dominate over the young. But there remains a conspicuous lack of stable dominance.

On the whole, chimpanzees are tolerant of one another in the group and of other groups. In contact with different species —so long as the outsider represents no threat—they are amicable. In the presence, for example, of baboon groups, the chimpanzees tend to ignore the other species. They do, however, react to sounds or gestures of alarm made by the baboons, by looking about to assure the safety of their own.

Communication is extensive. Goodall listed twenty-three distinct calls, each of which is characteristic of a particular circumstance. Other communication is affected by gesture, body posture, and facial expression.

Chimpanzee locomotion is effective. Movement on the ground is accomplished generally through the use of all four limbs, although upright stance is frequent. The chimp stands for better vision or to indicate interest or indignation. He may on occasion walk or run, rather efficiently, on his hindlimbs. Brachiation is utilized for short distances. Perhaps half to three-quarters of the chimpanzee day is spent in the trees, either feeding or resting, and for quick movement from branch to branch, the arms function efficiently.

The chimpanzee is primarily a vegetarian and spends from six to seven hours daily in feeding from the trees on fruit and leaves, which compose almost ninety per cent of the diet. The chimp seldom feeds extensively on the ground. Insects—ants and termites—provide a supplementary diet, and honey is eaten when obtainable. Eggs may or may not be eaten; some chimpanzees take them, shell and all, while others decline entirely.

The chimp must also be classified as carnivorous; meat is

eaten on occasion. Monkeys and bushpigs provide such a feast, and Goodall filmed the attack and kill of a small monkey by a band of male chimpanzees. There have been reports of chimpanzee seizure of human infants. One, grabbed from the mother's back, was recovered by natives, but the child died in the interval between chase and capture. Another, seized while left alone in a native camp, was recovered in a mutilated state. The West African police force reported to Goodall five other such cases. It is unclear whether the human infants were seized for food, but in each known case the child was mutilated, suggesting that they were indeed captured for feeding purposes.

Several instances of soil-feeding were observed; usually the soil taken was high in salt content. Drinking is done from streams, in a sucking rather than a lapping action.

Closely associated with the feeding function is the use of tools by chimpanzees. To obtain ants or termites, the chimp inserts a stick into the nest, leaving it there for a brief interval. After withdrawal, the chimp licks off the clinging insects. Honey is obtained in similar fashion. Stones are used to break apart the palm nut for the meat inside. Such tool use is noted elsewhere in the animal kingdom, but among chimpanzees, for the first time, actual tool-making has been observed. If a suitable stick is not available, the chimp is capable of modifying an unsuitable one by altering its length or shape.

Little is known of the life span of the native chimpanzee. In captivity, longevity has been recorded at between sixty and seventy years. No figures are available for chimps in their natural habitat, where predators exist, though in small number. The leopard is the only serious adversary. Man, of course, is the principle threat. Disease does not appear to be a great danger, though Goodall noted coughing, sneezing, and colds among the groups she observed. Broken limbs, fingers, and toes are common occurrences.

Travel is erratic and not at all extensive. The chimpanzee roams without apparent pattern in a constant forage for food, which appears to be available in sufficient amounts the year around. While the chimp sleeps in a different place each night, he remains in the same general area. New nests are constructed nightly, although occasionally a chimp may use a previous nest after covering it with new leaves or branches. Sleeping patterns are vague; chimpanzees generally sleep alone but near others of their group. Infants share the mother's nest, and on occasion, adult males and females may nest together.

Occasionally, "day nests" are hastily constructed for napping between feeding intervals. Nissen saw no day nests, but Goodall observed several, and the Reynolds study noted two ground nests. Generally the larger nests, used for night sleeping, are constructed about thirty to forty feet above the ground, near the food supply. No nests are found in the uppermost reaches, where fruit does not grow.

While numerous investigators have hypothesized mating seasons (at diverse times of the year), the female chimpanzee does have an estrus cycle. This cycle is approximately thirty-five days long, during which estrus, characterized by swelling and menstruation, occurs about the time of ovulation. Some observers have noted an increase in sexual activity for the months of August through November. However, pregnant females, newborn infants, and incidences of copulation at other times are frequent exceptions. It is probable, therefore, that copulation occurs in any month. Single births are the rule; these occur at intervals of not less than two and a half to three years.

In summary, the two most interesting points to evolve from recent studies are (1) that chimpanzees attack and kill relatively large animals for food, and (2) that tool-use is common among chimpanzees and tool-making does occur. For those who express surprise at the loose structural organization characteristic of the chimpanzee, Reynolds suggests the hypothesis that the chimpanzees possess a social organization so highly developed that it persists despite the characteristic fluidity of personnel. At this time, no reliable conclusion can be reached.

Suggested Readings

Carpenter, C. R.
1934. A field study of the behavior and social relations of howling monkeys. *Comp. Psychol. Monogr.*, 10(48):1–168.

1940. A field study in Siam of the behavior and social relations of the gibbon, *Hylobates lar. Comp. Psychol. Monogr.*, 16(5):1–212.

1964. *Naturalistic Behavior of Nonhuman Primates.* University Park, Pa.: Pa. State University Press.

DeVore, Irven
1963. A comparison of the ecology and behavior of monkeys and apes. *In: Classification and Human Evolution.* Viking Fund Publs. Anthrop. No. 7, pp. 3-1-19. Chicago: Aldine Publishing Co.

——— and S. L. Washburn
1963. Baboon ecology and human evolution. *In: African Ecology and Human Evolution.* Viking Fund Publs. Anthrop. No. 36, pp. 335–67. Chicago: Aldine Publishing Co.

Ferster, Charles B.
1964. Arithmetic behavior in chimpanzees. *Scientific American*, 210(5):98–106.

Goodall, J.
 1965. Chimpanzees of the Gombe Stream Reserve. *In:* Irven Devore (ed.), *Primate Behavior*. New York: Holt, Rinehart & Winston.
Kohler, W.
 1925. *The Mentality of Apes*. New York: Harcourt.
Reynolds, Vernon
 1965. Chimpanzees of the Budongo Forest. *In:* Irven Devore (ed.), *Primate Behavior*. New York: Holt, Rinehart & Winston.
Riopelle, Arthur J. and Paul A. Zahl.
 1967. Snowflake, the world's first white gorilla. *National Geographic* 131(3):443–48.
Schaller, George B.
 1964. *The Year of the Gorilla*. Chicago: University of Chicago Press.
Zuckerman, S.
 1932. *The Social Life of Monkeys and Apes*. London: Routledge and Kegan Paul, Ltd.

HEREDITY

chapter
10

In the preceding chapters, we have focused our attention primarily upon variation and development. In doing so, we have dealt with what is presently known from a *descriptive* viewpoint only. But what about those mechanisms that cause and control variation? How do species emerge through evolution over generations of time?

These questions bring us to the field of *genetics,* that study of heredity often described as the discipline that attempts to explain similarities and differences between related organisms. It is impossible to understand evolution and *speciation* (the development of new populations) without first knowing the basic genetic mechanisms that are constantly at work in the living organism. While neither student nor layman can claim to know genetics on the basis of this or any other single chapter, it is possible, by learning the basic genetic mechanisms, to gain an understanding of those areas pertinent to human populations.

Applications of Genetics

At the outset, we should know why, in addition to furthering our understanding of the evolutionary process, genetics comprises so integral a part of human biology. The knowledge gained through experimental plant and animal breeding and probing of the cellular structure must have application in daily living. What are these applications? Perhaps the most common utilization of genetic data is the improving of cultivated plants and domesticated animals. Genetic principles are also of use in the treatment of disease; because the predisposition for a particular affliction may be inheritable, knowledge of the hereditary history for the stricken individual contributes greatly toward his recovery and future well-being. In other cases—instances of disputed parentage, for example—genetic knowledge may have legal application.

Cellular Reproduction

Nineteenth-century scientists discovered that all organisms are communities of cells and, further, that every cell is the offspring of pre-existing cells. The genetics of any individual, then, begins with the process of reproduction. But not every organism reproduces itself in the same manner. Scientists have observed three basic types of reproduction:

Asexual, whereby a parent divides itself to form one or more offspring individuals. Chiefly confined to vegetative organisms, asexual reproduction consists of simple cellular division. In organisms employing this means of reproduction, there is no sexual differentiation between male and female.

Sexual, whereby there is a union of two specialized cells (*gametes*), one from each parent, to result in fertile offspring. From the male comes the *sperm;* from the female, the *ova,* or eggs.

Parthenogenesis, often termed "virgin birth," whereby the female cell does not require fertilization by the male cell. It is said, for example, that the male bee has never had a father and, although he may have millions of daughters, he will never have a son. The statement may sound ludicrous, but it is true. First, the *fertilized* eggs of the female bee develop into female offspring, the worker bees. The *unfertilized* eggs develop into males, the drones. The only function, then, of the male bee is to fertilize the queen in order to produce more workers, or female bees.

From this single example, it is clear that the male is not an absolute necessity among some forms of animal life. As a matter of fact, in rare instances—as in the case of the Oakgall wasp—no males exist. However, humans are products of *sexual* reproduction, and it is with this mode that we are primarily concerned.

Through sexual reproduction, the genetic make-up of any individual is determined equally by both parents. All the material which a human being inherits from his two parents is incorporated into the two gametes or sex cells: the ovum and the sperm. Fertilization occurs when the sperm penetrates the egg. At that point, the surface layer of the egg cell undergoes a change in which a fertilization membrane is formed, preventing fertilization by additional sperm, a vital prohibition since multiple fertilization does not lead to normal development.

The mature human body consists of trillions of cells. Each and every one of these cells is the offspring—created by repeated reproduction—of a single pair of gametes. The fusion of a male gamete (sperm) which a female gamete (ovum) produces the *zygote*, or fertilized egg. Within the nucleus of this zygote are the basic materials that explain the continuity of life forms, the continuation of characteristics from generation to generation, as well as the formation of differences. In order to understand how this is accomplished, we must turn to a brief discussion of the physical constituents of heredity.

The Physical Bases of Heredity

Each typical body cell contains an estimated 40,000 *genes*, those tiny units which dictate characteristics—brown eyes, for example, or straight hair. The genes in the body cells are of the same number and type as those present in the original zygote, from which the organism developed. The genes are made up of combinations of deoxyribonucleic acid (known commonly as DNA), ribonucleic acid (RNA), and several proteins. Hereditary determination in the genes results from variations in the molecular structure of the DNA.

As we have seen in Chapter 3, the genes in combination compose the chromosomes, those units which we are able to view under the microscope. The gene, however, is the unit responsible for variation. It can control cellular chemical synthesis; it can separate from its chromosome and "cross over" to another chromosome in the pair in a reproductive cell. Further, when its molecular structure changes (*mutates*), the gene can alter a single trait of a resulting cell or, in some cases, trait complexes. Traits in offspring cells result from the interaction between the genetic DNA code, passed on to control trait patterns in new cells, with the cellular environment and the pressures of the external environment which operate upon the organism. In simpler terms, gene patterns direct and control characteristics or traits but are limited by environmental factors.

Although we cannot yet be certain of the exact number of characteristic genes for a particular organism, we know from microscopic studies the characteristic number of chromosomes. Each species tends to have a constant number. For man, that number is 46, as compared with 78 for the dog or 200 for the crayfish. It was once believed that the chromosome number was related to the degree of evolutionary progress reached by a particular species: the higher the chromosome count, the more specialized or "advanced" the species. From the above figures, however, it should be clear that there is no relation between chromosome number and degree of specialization.

Mitosis

We have said that every cell grows out of pre-existing cells. But how, exactly, does the organism grow and develop? The answer lies in simple cellular reproduction; more specifically, in *mitosis,* the type of cell division which takes place in all body cells to produce two daughter cells from each single parent cell.

Microscopic investigations enable us to know in some detail the events of the mitotic process. These events are associated with a series of division steps, which may be followed in Figure 17.

During *interphase,* we see the cell "resting" between cell divisions. The chromosomes, located within the cellular nucleus, are at their greatest length. They bear at some specific point along their bodies a specialized structure known as a *centromere*, which functions to separate the chromosomes at a later stage of division. In higher animal cells and in some plant cells, there exists outside the nucleus (in the cytoplasm) a body called the *centrosome*, which features a central point (the *centriole*) and radiating "fibers" or particles which are collectively termed the *aster*.

At the outset of *prophase*, the genes are duplicated, initiating the process of mitosis. Immediately thereafter occurs chromosome duplication, but the centromeres do not follow suit at this time. We have, then, sets of duplicated chromosomes joined at a mutual centromere. The chromosomes become shortened and thickened, a step which can be viewed easily under the microscope. Duplication of the centromere follows.

Outside the cell nucleus, the centriole divides, and the two emerging centrioles move apart toward opposite directions, spreading between them the *spindle*, a network of fibers which appear with the movement of the centrioles. At this stage, the nuclear membrane begins to disappear and the chromosomes move toward the center of the spindle.

Metaphase begins when the chromosomes complete their journey to the central portion of the spindle. Here they line themselves up to form what is called the *equatorial plate*. The centromeres are now clearly duplicated; they move toward opposite ends of the cell, pulling the twin chromosomes apart so that they separate.

During *anaphase*, the chromosomes and the centromeres have completed movement toward opposite cell ends, in preparation for actual cell division.

Since *prophase*, the nuclear membrane has not been visible; it disappeared to permit movement of cellular components. Now, at *telophase* (terminal phase), new nuclear membranes appear at the end of the cell; they surround and envelop the chromosomes along with their genetic arrangement. The chromosomes themselves appear longer and thinner, resuming the form they exhibited during *interphase*. Simultaneously, there develops along the center of the cell a deep furrow, which soon

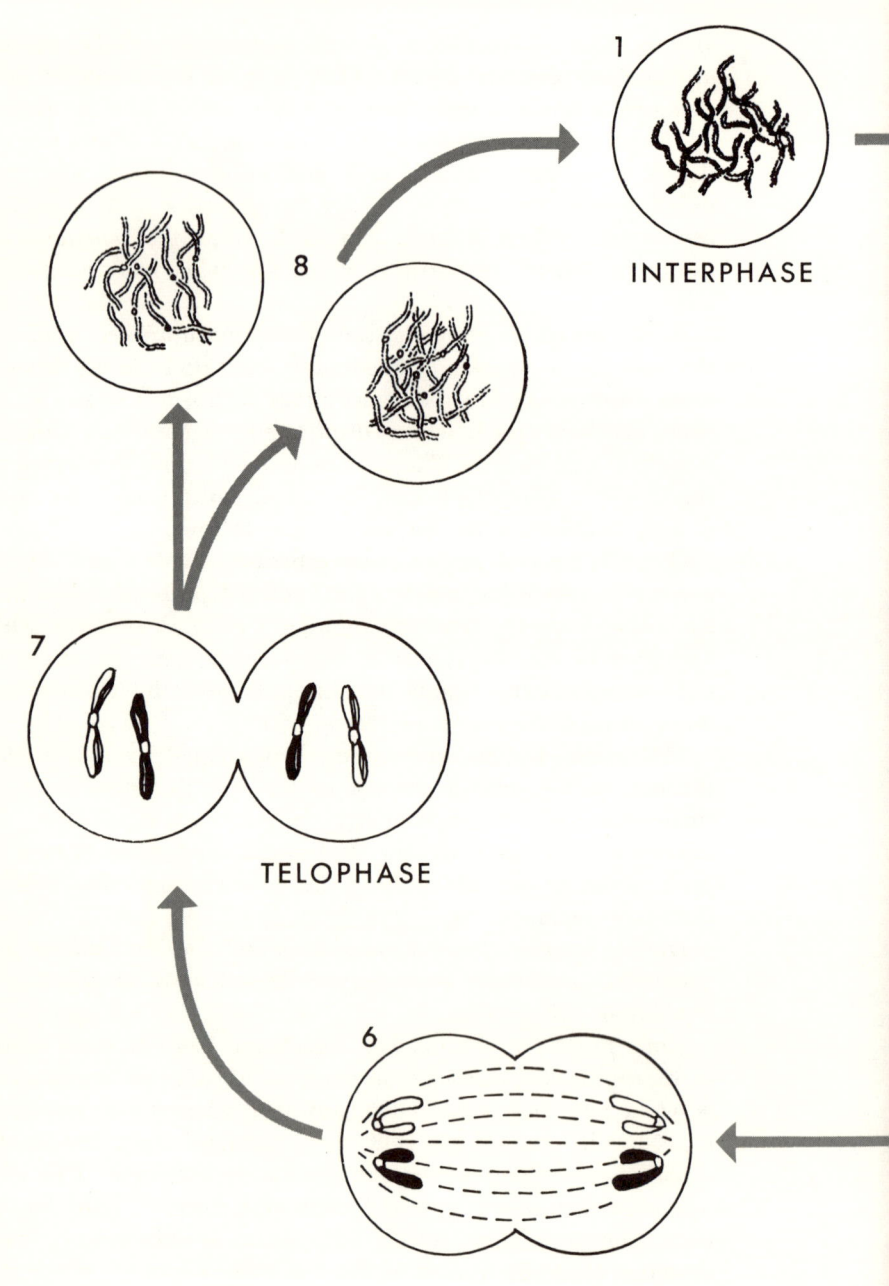

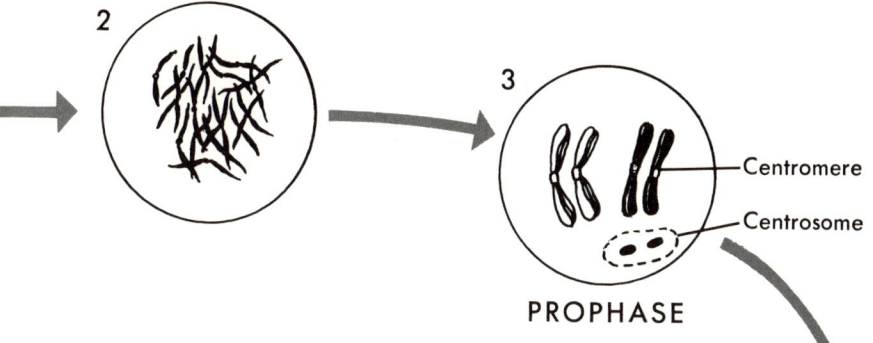

FIGURE 17 Mitosis. In this schematic representation, we see the cell (1) in *interphase*. In (2) the cell's chromosomes are duplicated and become short and thick, easily visible under the microscope. Outside the nucleus (3), the centriole begins to divide, and moves (4) to opposite cell ends to form the aster and spindle. With *metaphase* (4), the chromosomes line up at the center of the elongated cell. In *anaphase* (5), the chromosomes have moved to opposite cell ends, in preparation for actual cell division. At *telophase* (6), new nuclear membranes begin to appear, surrounding (7) the chromosomes. In (8), the daughter cells, division complete, rest in the *interphase* condition, ready for a new division.

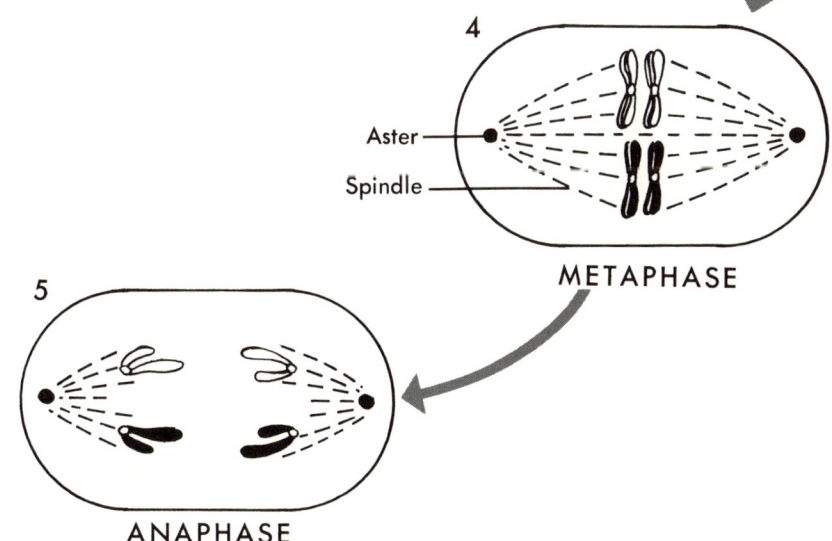

constricts to effect actual cell division. The result is the formation of two daughter cells, each in an interphase condition, with the appropriate number of cellular and genetic constituents. The chromosome count, of course, is constant.

It is the mitotic process which permits growth of the organism, producing in each cell chromosomes in *exact replica* of those in the parent cell. This process is repeated in all of the trillions of cells that eventually form the mature organism. There is, however, one exception: the production of sex cells. These—the gametes—go through a specialized process of reproduction termed *meiosis*.

Meiosis

We have seen from the foregoing discussion that in mitosis, daughter cells receive the exact number of chromosomes as were present in the original cell. We know too that for each species, there is a characteristic chromosome count. Keeping in mind that in sexual reproduction, there is a fusion of *two* cells in fertilization to produce the zygote, how can we explain the constancy of the chromosome number for each species? The answer lies in the mechanics of meiosis, a specialized cell division which results in the formation of cells with only half the usual complement of chromosomes. The resulting daughter cells are the gametes, any of which may fuse with a gamete of the opposite sex to produce an entirely new individual with the normal complement of chromosomes.

In the male, meiosis (see Figure 18) is termed *spermatogenesis* and results in the formation of the spermatozoa, or sperm. This process takes place in the testes and occurs continuously from maturity (sexual maturity in man is reached during puberty). At any time, under normal conditions, the mature male maintains a normal level of 150 to 200 million sperm cells.

Meiosis proceeds in much the same manner as mitosis, except that in the former process, there are two divisions rather than one. During prophase in meiosis, the duplicated chromosomes pair. This pairing (termed *synapsis*) results in the formation, at telophase, of daughter cells each of which carries *twenty-three double* chromosomes.

The second division, which immediately follows the first, is termed *reduction division* because it permits separation of the double chromosomes. The resultant daughter cells (four in number) each carry twenty-three *single* chromosomes. In other words, four spermatids have been created, each with the *haploid* (half) number of chromosomes rather than the *diploid* (full, or usual) number. The diploid number is not restored until fusion of the sperm with an ovum, in conception of a new individual. The characteristic shape of the sperm cell results from a condensation of nuclear material to form the head. The tail, which trails behind, is useful in locomotion.

In the female, meiosis is termed *oogenesis,* or egg formation. It takes place in the ovary and is ordinarily accomplished before birth, so that an approximate 500,000 eggs reside in the ovary through puberty, one ripening each month thereafter. Of these, only about four hundred—during a usual thirty-year period of childbearing potential—have a chance to participate in the creation of a new individual. The process of meiosis in the female is so similar to that in the male that it is not necessary to outline here the oogenetic process. The results are identical: four daughter cells, each with the haploid number of chromosomes.

The ovum is larger in size than the sperm. This, however, serves to provide a supply of food for the developing embryo. Despite the disparity in size, each parent contributes equally. When the sperm and the egg (each in haploid condition) unite, there occurs fertilization, which restores the haploid condition. The fertilized egg (zygote) carries the full complement of chromosomes; for man, forty-six. And now mitosis occurs, repeatedly, enabling the zygote to develop from a single cell into a whole and functioning multicellular individual.

Sex Determination

We have seen that in fertilization, the diploid number of chromosomes is restored. In other words, the twenty-three chromosomes carried by the sperm unite with the twenty-three chromosomes carried by the ovum, to total forty-six chromosomes in all. The two sets of chromosomes join in *homologous*

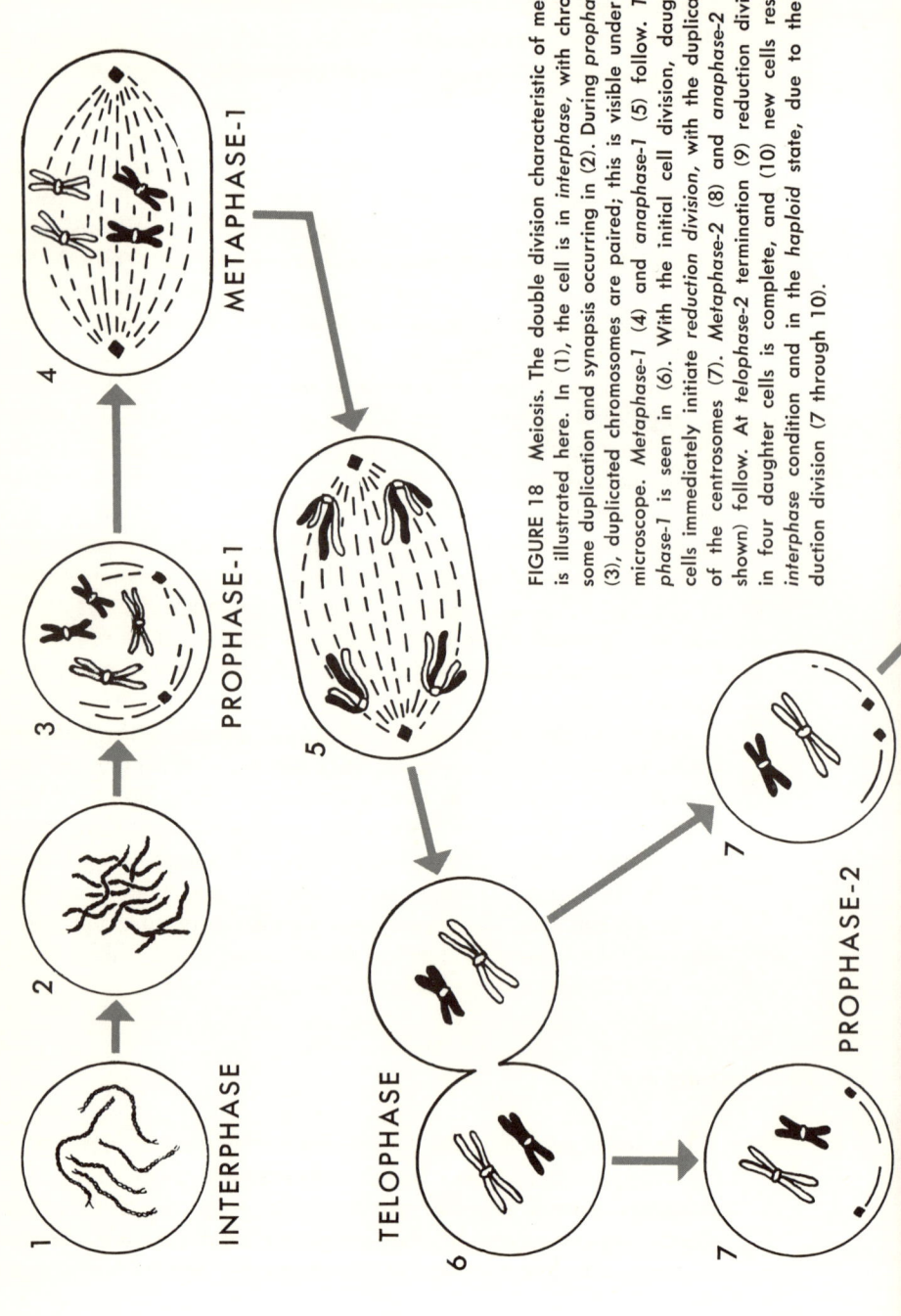

FIGURE 18 Meiosis. The double division characteristic of meiosis is illustrated here. In (1), the cell is in *interphase*, with chromosome duplication and synapsis occurring in (2). During *prophase-1* (3), duplicated chromosomes are paired; this is visible under the microscope. *Metaphase-1* (4) and *anaphase-1* (5) follow. *Telophase-1* is seen in (6). With the initial cell division, daughter cells immediately initiate reduction division, with the duplication of the centrosomes (7). *Metaphase-2* (8) and *anaphase-2* (not shown) follow. At *telophase-2* termination (9) reduction division in four daughter cells is complete, and (10) new cells rest in *interphase* condition and in the *haploid* state, due to the reduction division (7 through 10).

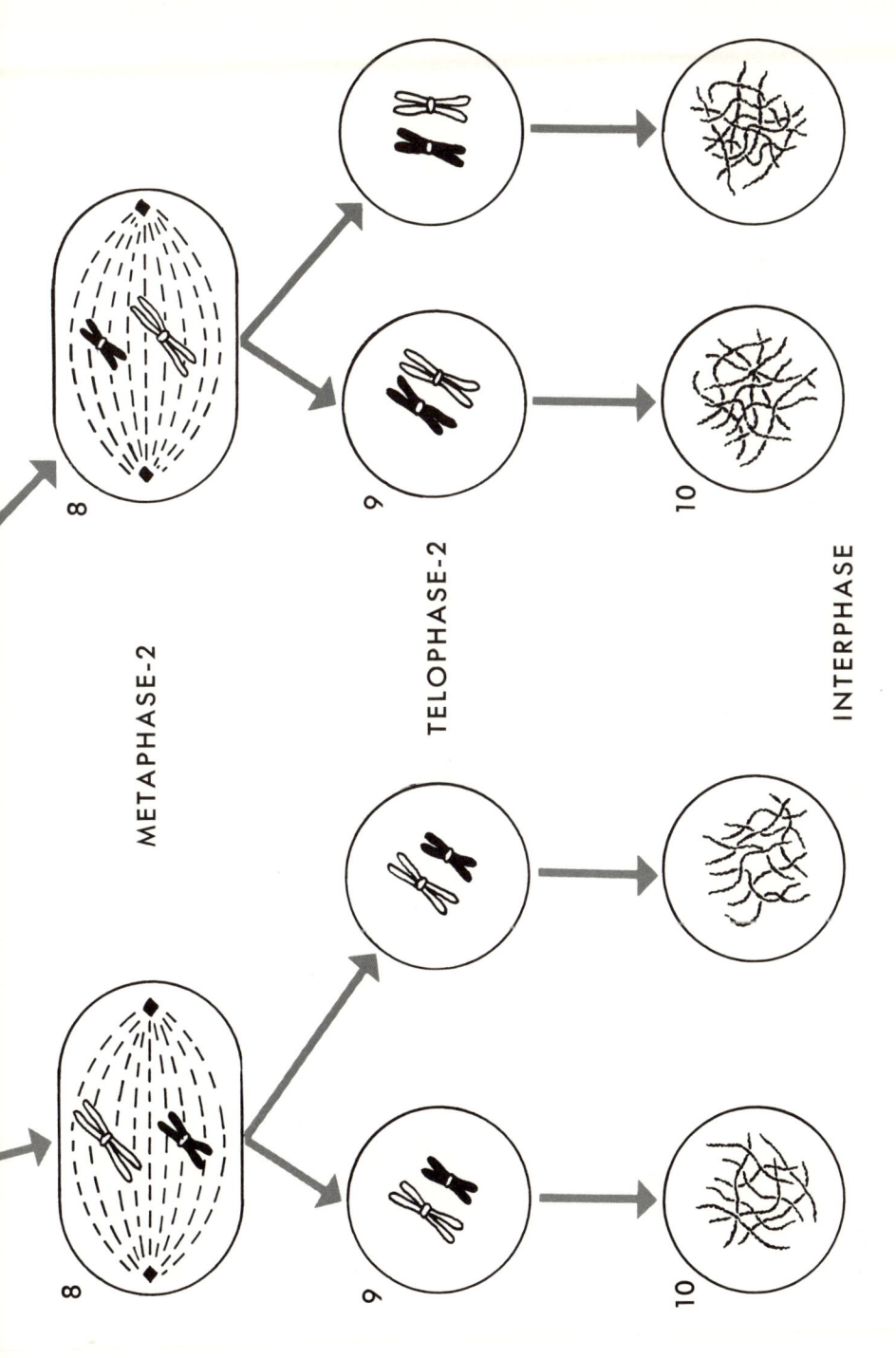

(structurally similar) pairs, with a single exception: in the male, there is one pair that are not perfect mates. In the female, all twenty-three "twin chromosomes" match. Therefore, geneticists have learned that it is the twenty-third pair of chromosomes which determine the sex of offspring.

The twenty-third pair are termed *sex chromosomes* or *allosomes*. For the sake of convenience when discussing sex determination, the other matched pairs are termed autosomes; they do not relate to sex. We use an alphabetical shorthand in order to refer to the allosomes. In the female, the allosomes are written XX. In the male, we refer to the allosomes as XY, thus indicating the differences between the members of that pair.

During meiosis, the sex chromosomes are separated so that each male gamete receives either an X chromosome or a Y chromosome. The female gametes all receive X chromosomes, because no Y form is found for the female. When the diploid condition is restored at fertilization, the sex of the resulting offspring depends upon whether the X female gamete combines with the X male gamete (resulting in a female offspring) or with the Y gamete (resulting in a male offspring). It is therefore the father rather than the mother who determines the sex of their child, a fact to be kept in mind by those anxious fathers who are disappointed in their wives for producing a daughter when a son was desired, or vice-versa.

Dominance

Mendel's experiments, cited in Chapter 3, illustrate the principles of dominance. Almost all characters or traits show two or more different forms or alternative expressions. Features subject to dominance, for example, are eye color or hair form. As a rule, the two or more different expressions of the same character are mutually exclusive; that is, an individual shows one or the other. When two individuals mate, each differing in regard to a single unit character, their offspring will show either one or the other of these character expressions. Assume that a black guinea pig and a white guinea pig were mated. Offspring were black. In this case, black *dominates* over white, for that character which appears in the first generation, to the exclusion of alternate expressions, is *dominant*. The character which does not appear is termed *recessive*. In this example, white is recessive to black.

In some cases, there is an absence of dominance, resulting in an intermediate expression between two alternative characters. The classic example for this phenomenon is seen in the mating of white and black Andalusian chickens; the heterozygous offspring are neither white nor black, but a steel-blue color.

We have seen, again in Chapter 3, that in reproduction, the members of each pair of genes segregate out so that just one of every two paired genes is transmitted from each parent to each offspring. The genes work in pairs, one from each parent. These are termed *alleles*, the alternative forms which demonstrate a reciprocal dominant-recessive relationship between two homologous genes.

Therefore, although the contributions from the parents are equal, the effects are not. In our example citing guinea pigs, the white parent contributed genetically in the same degree as did the black parent. But the resulting offspring were black.

Genotype-Phenotype

There are two ways to consider an individual, as we have noted. We may look at the *phenotype* (that combination of characters which make up the physical appearance of the individual) or at the *genotype* (the genetic potential of the individual which is carried in the cells but which cannot be seen). We can, however, *infer* the genetic potential in many cases and in a number of ways. Utilizing genetic shorthand once more, let:

AA = Dominant normal (homozygous)
Aa = Dominant normal (heterozygous)
aa = Recessive abnormal (homozygous)

Each single character refers to the gene inherited from one parent. Consistent with Mendel's theories, AA, the dominant normal, is homozygous because the combined genes are alike;

Aa is also considered dominant normal because *phenotypically* it will express the dominant character form of the gene A, but it is heterozygous in that the two genes differ. The recessive, as we have seen, appears phenotypically only in the absence of a dominant allele; thus aa is recessive abnormal and is homozygous because the paired genes are alike. An example of recessive abnormal inheritance among humans is *albinism,* the genetically determined inability to produce the basic color pigment. Assume that a homozygous dominant normal male (AA) mates with a homozygous recessive abnormal female (aa) who is an albino:

$$(AA)(aa) = (Aa)(Aa)(Aa)(Aa)$$

All offspring are heterozygous, but appear phenotypically normal, for the normal condition (A) is dominant. Then assume that two individuals, both dominant normal and heterozygous for albinism (both Aa) mate:

$$(Aa)(Aa) = (AA)(Aa)(Aa)(aa)$$

Keeping in mind that we are dealing with a hypothetical case in order to demonstrate genetic *potential* only, the following offspring are noted in genetic shorthand above: three phenotypically normal (one homozygous normal, two heterozygous normal) and one phenotypically and genotypically abnormal (recessive abnormal). Therefore, of the four hypothetical children, the fourth would inherit the inability to produce basic color pigment; in other words, an albino child would be born of two phenotypically normal parents.

Sex Linkage

Simple dominant-recessive inheritance shows no association with either sex, as in the case of albinism, where either parent might carry the potential for producing a recessive abnormal offspring. There was apparent a random relation only. However, there are certain diseases that differ between the sexes, and the appearance of the trait expressing such a disease is dependent upon whether it is handed down by the father or by the mother. This phenomenon was understood only after the discovery of the sex chromosomes, when it was found that the twenty-third pair, in the male, consisted of differing component members. Therefore, concerning the genes located in the sex chromosomes, it is to be expected that the two sexes should not be hereditarily equivalent.

The traits which are based on such genes are called *sex-linked* and their mode of transmission is termed *sex-linked inheritance.* Obviously, there are two types of such inheritance: X-linked inheritance and Y-linked inheritance. These should not be confused with traits which are *sex-limited*—those which are determined by autosomal alleles. For example, voice traits (tenor, baritone, bass) are sex-limited; they are expressed differently in the two sexes even though the genes are present in both males and females. And they are under the partial control of body hormones.

A rather dramatic example of Y-linked inheritance is found in the case of the "porcupine man," a history—while not too reliably documented—which illustrates graphically the effects of Y-linked inheritance. In 1717, two apparently normal English parents bore an apparently normal son. At the age of seven to eight weeks, however, the child's skin began to yellow and blacken, eventually thickening until his entire body was covered with thick rough scales and cylindrical bristle-like outgrowth of about an inch in length. Ed Lambert was the first known "porcupine man."

As an adult, Lambert had six sons, all of whom were similarly afflicted. For four generations, *all* the sons born in the Lambert line exhibited the effects of this peculiar disease, but the daughters were not affected. Making the best of a bad arrangement, the Lambert men turned to the sideshow circuit, becoming famous circus people. The disease apparently rose from a mutation (a spontaneous change resulting from a physical or chemical change in gene structure) and was passed on from generation to generation, carried only on the Y chromosome so that only male descendants expressed the trait.

Other, less repugnant traits known to be Y-linked are *hypertrichosis* (characterized by the growth of long black hairs from the ears) and webbed toes (seen between the second and third digits). In either case, as in the case of the porcupine disease, only males inherit and transmit the traits, for the females receive no Y chromosomes.

The situation is rather different for X-linked traits, for while the female never receives the Y chromosome, the male receives one Y and one X. Therefore, he participates in X-linkage. Consider the example of red-green color blindness. For females, the normal condition is dominant, so that if a woman inherits the heterozygous condition (Cc), her vision will not be affected. She is color-blind for red and green *only* if she inherits the recessive homozygous condition (cc). The male does not fare so well. Keeping in mind that in the human male, the twenty-third chromosome pair differs in size and character, the male cannot offset the X-linked gene for red-green color blindness with a homologous gene for the normal condition. Therefore, while a female must receive two recessive genes in order for this condition to be expressed, the male will be afflicted with a single recessive gene on the affected X chromosome. He has no homologous gene—of normal or abnormal potential—with which to counteract the potential for the affliction.

The same is true in the case of hemophilia, another X-linked disease. Hemophilia is sometimes called the "bleeder disease," because its victims suffer delayed coagulation of blood, leading to excessive bleeding and/or spontaneous hemorrhage. This is the disease which plagued the Spanish royal family for generations. The male who inherits the recessive X chromosome carrying the trait for hemophilia again has no homologous chromosome with which to offset the effects of the X-linked gene. In this case, however, it is the female who bears the burden of greater danger: generally, the female hemophiliac will not survive her first menses.

Mutations

We have discussed the transmission of traits from one generation to another and have noted that it is this transmission which promotes variation through a sexual recombination of genes, as seen in our earlier discussion of Mendelian principles of assortment. But other variations occur also, these as a result of internal changes in the molecular structure of the genes themselves. This happens when there is an alteration of the DNA code, that means by which the gene controls cell growth. If these variations are so stable that they are transmitted to offspring, they are termed *mutations*.

Scientists have estimated that the frequency of mutation is one for every 100,000 genes. An overwhelming majority of mutations are detrimental; these are the ones which—while they may not even be visible—cause some decrease in viability (capacity for survival) or fertility when expressed. Some mutated genes are *lethal;* that is, their effect is so extreme as to cause the death of a homozygous organism. This results, of course, in the elimination of that gene, for the organism so affected does not survive to reproduce. The number of lethal genes, however, remains more or less stable, for as the expressed lethals are eliminated through death or infertility, new lethal mutations continue to appear.

If the mutant gene is recessive, the generation in which it occurs will express no visible trait effect, and the mutant effects will be expressed in quite low frequencies in later generations in homozygous genotypes. If, however, the mutant gene is dominant and not lethal, it will be expressed phenotypically at once. And the smaller the gene pool (the genes of all members of a breeding population), the more widespread will be the effects of the mutant gene. This is why marriage between family members is discouraged; the chance of producing offspring homozygous for detrimental traits increases as the available gene pool decreases in size.

There is, of course, potential value in mutations, particularly to plant- and animal-breeders. The navel orange is an example of a mutation product which was noted and propagated. The seedless grape is another. Geneticists therefore have devoted much attention to the artificial induction of mutations. It was early discovered that exposure to X ray greatly increased mutation rates. Chemical induction is another means, and it has been found that such chemicals as mustard, nitrogen, phenol, and formaldehyde produce positive results. Unfortunately, a number of these have also been found to be *carcinogenic* (cancer-producing). Also effective in raising mutation rates have been ultra-violet rays. But what are the *natural* causes of mutation?

The answer is pure speculation. Some experts believe that exposure to natural radiation induces mutation, but from experiments with the fruitfly, it has been found that normal radiation levels are not sufficient to explain the frequency of mutant genes existing in known populations. The answer most probably lies within the cell, with a substitution of some chemical in the replication of DNA, or energy fluctuations resulting in rearrangement of the DNA chain. There has been no conclusive evidence to date to support either thesis.

Populations and Gene Pools

We have spoken of the *gene pool*, the whole of genes available in all members of a breeding population. We might further refer to a *Mendelian population*, which is considered to be a localized grouping of individuals of a given species which interbreed among themselves and occasionally with neighboring populations. Within a breeding population, the gene pool provides a reservoir of genes available to the population for the next generation, and because the human reproductive processes tend to stabilize the available genetic material, each succeeding generation tends to inherit a relatively unchanged gene pool. This fact works against evolution, for genetic change is the key to evolutionary progress. What factors, then, tend to upset the genetic equilibrium for the breeding population?

Mutation, as we have seen, produces change. The smaller the gene pool, the greater are the effects of this change. Natural selection, discussed earlier in this volume, is another important factor in the evolutionary process, constantly at work to reject unfavorable variations and preserve those that lend viability to the individual and to the species.

But there are other selective factors at work. In the human society, cultural patterns limit or differentiate reproduction. For example, many human societies express a social preference for exogamous marriage; that is, a member of that society is expected to marry *outside* his own community. The effect, while most frequently unknown to those who practice the custom, is to bring in new genetic potential, additions to the population's gene pool. Other examples are limitless.

Population mixture—the merging of two distinct populations—produces the same effect in greater degree, resulting in new combinations of genes in succeeding generations. This is *hybridization;* often, the hybrid has greater survival potential or greater fertility than either of the contributing populations. And, of course, a new phenotype is born. Eventually this new phenotype may result in a new taxonomic type, as in the case of the American Negro.

It is also possible that a small population may experience change without the impetus provided by mutation or selection. When this occurs, we term the phenomenon *genetic drift.* Genetic drift among human populations most commonly occurs in small groups, with the accidental increase or decrease of genetic elements. One example is seen in the departure of splinter groups, which may reduce the gene frequency for a particular trait. Other examples could be cited, but the relevant point has been made: with genetic drift, change in the gene pool is effected in the absence of any change in original gene structure.

The basis for evolution, then, is the genetic potential of the individual and of the group, worked upon by external factors of environment and accident or induced change.

Suggested Readings

Bonner, David M. and Stanley E. Mills
    1964. *Heredity* (2d ed.). Englewood Cliffs, N.J.: Prentice-Hall, Inc.

Dobzhansky, T. and G. Allen
    1966. Does natural selection continue to operate in modern mankind? *In:* Thomas W. McKern (ed.), *Readings in Physical Anthropology,* pp. 71–81. Englewood Cliffs, N.J.: Prentice-Hall, Inc.

Spuhler, J. N. (ed.)
    1967. *Genetic Diversity and Human Behavior.* Viking Fund Publs. Anthrop. No. 45. Chicago: Aldine.

Swanson, Carl P.
    1964. *The Cell* (2d ed.). Englewood Cliffs, N.J.: Prentice-Hall, Inc.

HUMAN VARIATION

chapter
11

We have seen in earlier chapters that all of modern mankind is grouped collectively within a single species. From our discussion of taxonomy, we know that this is a sound grouping, for all living members of *Homo sapiens sapiens* share numerous traits which distinguish them from all other organisms. But obviously man's taxonomic classification is *polytypic;* that is, it involves numerous types, and therefore there are many discrete biological groupings beyond the specific level. Some are obvious to any observer, while others are more difficult to distinguish; these groups are generally included under the catch-all term *race*.

The anthropologist hesitates to use the word *race* for numerous and valid reasons. First, the term has been linked with other kinds of groups. We speak, for example, of the French race, the Jewish race, or the Aryan race, when we should more properly refer to the French nationality, the Jewish religion, or the Aryan language. Certainly there are times when biological designations may coincide with linguistic, religious, or national boundaries, but this is not the proper application of the term. Race is a *biological* concept, and races are *biological* units.

Many people still think of race in terms of a few "pure" races, and this attitude leads to racial typing of individuals by criteria other than biological. In early attempts to classify individuals within racial categories, the results often assigned individual family members to diverse racial classifications.

Further, the term *race* carries with it certain undesirable connotations, which lead too often to oppression or discrimination. But it is the obligation of the anthropologist not only to investigate, but also to make himself heard—and understood—within his own society. In order to do so, he uses the language available to him, speaking in terms accepted and understood by the people of his own culture. And he is stuck, unfortunately, with the word *race*.

Nevertheless, he can qualify that term. For our purposes, we shall define *race* as *a breeding population that is distinguished from other breeding populations within the species in the frequency of certain hereditary traits*. Ideally, the race concept is a matter of estimating the genotype. In most instances, however, we depend upon our increasing knowledge of the phenotype, inferring a basic genotypic differentiation.

Our emphasis on the physical should not be interpreted as a refutation of the cultural influence. Man is both biological and social; cultural factors may figure prominently in the formation or maintenance of a given trait.

Studies with Comparative Populations

But why study race at all, when rational men are striving toward human unity? We compare human populations, of course, in order to trace historical relationships. Because generations are linked physically through gene transmission, we hope to analyze the genetic composition of various groups of mankind. We utilize comparative studies also to reinforce and better illuminate the mechanics of evolution. Further, we want to learn more about the effects on man of diverse environments. And we apply data gleaned from disease-incidence studies in an attempt to further control or cure numerous human diseases. Through investigations in the field, we can build a complete classification of the human populations of the world and thus contribute to taxonomic methodology. And if for no other reason, we study race because man as a social animal is incurably romantic: like a mountain climber, the anthropologist is unable to resist the challenge of the unknown. This is *our* species, and, as men, we are fascinated by man.

Tools in Human Variation

We start by looking at some of the traits that have been used to classify races or various breeding populations. Some are phenotypic, others genotypic. In any case, they reflect human variation in numerous ways: stature, configuration, and other bodily measurements; skin color; hair color and form; eye color and form; dental anomalies; blood types; characteristic diseases or predisposition to such diseases.

Anthropometry

It is difficult to express differences in body size and shape. For this reason, we rely heavily upon *anthropometry*, the scientific measurement of the human body. Such measurement is no simple matter; it requires a set of standardized techniques, and application with meticulous attention to detail. Landmarks, whether on flesh or on bone, must be clearly defined and precisely located. Instruments utilized must be accurate. Any deviation arising from faulty instruments or technique precludes use of obtained data in correlation with that obtained from other observers.

Anthropometry is too wide and too complex a field of inquiry to discuss in detail here, but we can touch upon a few examples. As we have seen, easily visible landmarks are requisite. These are always related to bone and are ideally fixed. Measurements on skeletal material, of course, are always more precise, for layers of muscle and adipose tissue impedes localization of the landmarks. Utilizing many instruments (including both sliding and spreading calipers, anthropometers, flexible steel tape, and countless others) we undertake to measure the head and body in as complete and precise manner as possible, recording such data as overall height and weight; head height, length, and breadth; facial height; nasal height and breadth; chest circumference; length of hand, forearm, and upper arm; total upper extremity length; length of thigh, lower leg, and foot; total lower extremity length; sitting height; pelvic breadth, and so on. This data is applied to one or more of the numerous available indices, permitting more coherent and concise expression of results. The indices always take into consideration the differences between the two sexes; that is, female indices are available separately from male indices.

The *cephalic index* provides an illustration of how measurements are used in racial classification. Given the measurements for head breadth and length, the investigator obtains the cephalic index by multiplying the maximum head breadth by 100, then dividing this figure by the maximum head length. The resulting figure expresses the breadth as a percentage of the length, and is then applied to a standard classification, the simplest of which is that designed by Vallois [1] as follows:

dolichocephalic	up to 75.9
mesocephalic	76.0–80.9
brachycephalic	81.0+

Among the populations whose cephalic indices most frequently fall within the brachycephalic (round-headed) range are the Lapps and Armenians. Typical dolichocephalics (long-headed individuals) are the Masai of Africa, the Micronesians, and the Eskimos of Labrador.

Of course, the Vallois classification is one of many. Other indices are utilized similarly, but measurement alone does not

[1] Vallois, Henri V., Technique anthropométrique. *La Semaine des Hôpitaux de Paris*, No. 13, 10 pp. 18 février, 1948.

constitute racial classification. In many instances, shape or configuration, color, biochemistry, or congenital anomalies aid in the classification of man at the subspecies level.

Skin Color or Pigmentation

Skin color has long been used to distinguish different peoples. For instance, we know that the ancient Egyptians made such a distinction; in art, they represented themselves in flesh tones while picturing their neighbors in other colors. The people from the upper Nile region were typically coloured black, while the Libyans were painted red. To a certain extent, we can say that this represents an early acknowledgement of human variation based on phenotypic identification.

We know that the basic pigment substance is *melanin,* a chemically complex material microscopically visible in granular form. The melanin-forming properties are controlled by genes; we do not know, however, whether a single gene or a gene complex is involved, although we suspect multiple gene control. Normal skin color is the result of several factors operating upon the genetic potential. Light, for instance, is absorbed in the melanin granules located in the epidermis.

Major color differences are due to the number of melanin granules present; the higher the number, the darker the skin appears to be. Anything that adheres to the skin—including dirt—will affect skin color. There have been many attempts in history to change the color of the skin, but most of these are short-lived. Bleaching, for example, does not last long, as the outer cells slough off normally. Tanning, best exemplified in our own sun-hungry culture, will darken the skin temporarily. The only permanent way to alter skin color is through tattooing, the insertion of pigment into lower skin layers. This will not be affected by later replacement of cells on the outer surface of the skin. The tattoo, once done, is there to stay, often to the regret of its wearer but, again, often to his delight.

There are, of course, normal changes in skin color. With aging, an individual's skin becomes spotty for causes unknown. Pregnancy results in a number of localized changes (in the areola of the female breast, for instance). And there are changes due to the temporary increase of melanin granules, as in tanning, when ultraviolet stimulates the production of melanin. Some individuals, however, do not react to this stimulus: the true albino, probably occurring in all present races, burns rather than tans on prolonged exposure to the sun, because his skin lacks the protecting melanin.

There is an amazing range of color among the world's populations and, significantly, among localized populations. We have chromatic scales in which shades within each basic color range are graduated and numbered, permitting expression of the color in numeric terms. Such expression requires accurate and standardized instruments, as well as a discriminating eye for skin tones.

Hair Color

Hair color results from the presence within the hair shaft of melanin (with black to yellow-brown properties) and lipochromes (offering red-gold effects). The red element is masked, in the hair of most people, by a greater amount of melanin. Chromatic scales are utilized here also for measurement, with four basic color shades recognized, as opposed to the thirty-four to over three hundred recognized for skin color.

Eye Pigmentation

Eye color depends upon the presence of melanin concentrations in two layers of the iris. When the inner pigmented layer of the eye is exposed, the eye appears to be blue, while the darker shades result from the outer pigmented layers. Chromatic scales are utilized here, too, for measurement of any individual or population, with the exception of the albino, which is not represented. Since the albino lacks melanin, he is considered an anomaly, not representative of any particular group.

Genetically controlled, eye color demonstrates a dominance in the darker shades. Mutation is probably responsible for the lighter color so obvious in the populations of northern Europe.

Hair Form

Hair form is also genetically controlled, although differences in configuration are not very well understood at present. Normally, form is expressed as straight, wavy, curly, or coiled, with a complex range of gradations in between, and may be influenced by external factors. High fever may produce new hair forms or result in hair loss, partial or total. Pregnancy may bring the same effects. We are speaking here of head hair, but body hair is also relevant and is used as another criterion in classifying man. *Hirsute* populations are those whose members exhibit considerable body hair (the Melanesians, for example); *glabrous* populations are those with little or no body hair (the American Indians, the African Bushmen).

Eye Form

The Mongoloid populations are most easily identified by eye shape; they possess the *epicanthic fold* (often termed *Mongolian fold*). In many groups of Asia and among the American Indians, there occurs a skin fold over the upper eyelid. Among non-Mongoloid groups, the eyelid opening is horizontal, lacking the fold which lends an angled appearance.

Dentition

Also typical of the Mongoloid groups is the presence of what is termed the *shovel-shaped incisor,* a tooth typically concave from the lingual (tongue) side and with prominent lateral borders. Found in many races, the incidence of shovel-shaping is highest among the group noted, substantiating the theory for Asiatic population of the New World, as American Indian groups demonstrate a high frequency of shovel-shaping.

Blood Types

Almost everyone knows that human blood may be typed or classified, but such a practice has a relatively short history. The first known blood transfusion took place in 1492 A.D., when Pope Innocent VIII, wanting to live longer, transfused blood from two vigorous young males. The experiment was unsuccessful: all died. We have no way of knowing whether the outcome resulted from a problem of incompatible type or from infection.

Whatever the reason, blood transfusions were banned by law in the late seventeenth century, and investigations ceased for a time. Then, early in the present century came the discovery of four different blood types, designated as I, II, III, and IV. Investigators found that the serum or fluid part of the blood of certain humans had the ability to cause clumping or clotting of the red blood cells of other normal human bloods. Action depended upon types combined.

Later the types were renamed, in a system we now refer to as the ABO Blood System. Blood type does not result from single-factor inheritance but from the action of multiple alleles. Both A and B are dominant over O, but A and B can also be present together (AB). In other words, two different blood characteristics, A and B, may be present singly, present in combination, or absent entirely, in which case the type is designated as O.

Blood types were established on the basis of reactions observed in mixtures of blood from different persons. Essentially, these reactions occur between the red blood cells of one individual and the serum from another individual, and the reactions are termed *agglutination*. When blood is mixed, one of two possible results can be observed: either red blood cells are normally distributed in the serum, or the red cells clump together.

In order to understand this phenomenon, we look to the reason for these two possible reactions. The red cells of an individual possess either one or the other of two substances, or both, or neither: Antigen A and Antigen B. At the same time, the serum of the same individual possesses either one or the other of two substances, or both, or neither: Antibody A and

Antibody B. The red cells containing Antigen A are agglutinated by *A* antibodies, and cells containing Antigen B are agglutinated by *B* antibodies. That is, the antigens are agglutinated by the antibodies.

Whole blood can be transfused safely only between members of the same blood group. However, if necessary, it is possible to use certain other combinations because (1) antibodies in the fluid part of a pint of transfused blood are partially absorbed by the tissues of an incompatible recipient before they can agglutinate the red cells, and (2) those antibodies not absorbed are diluted by the large volume of the recipient's serum.

In order to prevent failure, we adhere to certain transfusion rules, utilizing the terms "universal donor" (O) and "universal recipient" (AB). Group O blood lacks antigens in its red corpuscles; since it is the antigens which are agglutinated by the antibodies, and no antigens are present in Group O blood, type O blood may be donated universally; that is, to all blood types. The "universal recipient," Type AB, lacks antibodies in its serum and therefore cannot agglutinate the red corpuscles donated by any other type. Theoretically, then, Group AB individuals can receive blood of any type.

Table IV indicates possible blood donors and recipients. Group A possesses antigens A and antibodies B, while Group B possesses antigens B and antibodies A. Group O, which lacks antigens, possesses in serum antibodies A and B, while Group AB, which lacks antibodies, possesses antigens AB in the red corpuscles.

TABLE IV

Type Chart of Feasible Blood Donors and Recipients

Blood Type	May Receive Types	May Donate To
A	A, O	A, AB
B	B, O	B, AB
AB	ALL	AB
O	O	ALL

Most genetic causes of abnormal development of the unborn child reside either in the mother or the child. Certain congenital abnormalities, however, have been shown to arise from the mutual interaction of maternal and filial genotypes. The foremost of these interactions is related to the now-famous *Rh locus*. The Rh factor is inherited; Rh positive is dominant over Rh negative. An abnormality may occur when the mother has an Rh negative factor and the fetus an Rh positive factor. During the prenatal period, the placenta acts as a barrier to retard passage of harmful substances to the developing fetus. The mother's blood supply does not circulate through the body of the fetus, but does penetrate the placental barrier to carry food and other elements into the fetal blood system. A mother who has been sensitized to Rh positive blood, either through transfusions or through a rupture in the placenta during a previous birth will develop antibodies against Rh positive blood. And since the blood systems of the mother and child are in such close contact, these antibodies can destroy the red blood cells of the fetus. When this happens, the condition of abnormality is termed *erthroblastosis fetalis,* an anemia due to the hemolysis (destruction) of fetal blood cells. The condition may lead to abortion or stillbirth. This is the reason for the famous Coomb's test, performed regularly to ascertain whether such a condition is likely to arise. The test itself has doubtless saved many lives and should be performed at the outset of pregnancy when the mother is known to possess the Rh negative factor.

There are numerous blood systems in addition to the ABO group: the S, MN, Rh, P, Duffy, Hunter, Lewis, Lutheran, and others. They are relevant, but time and space prohibits a full consideration of each at this point. We are primarily concerned now in applying our knowledge of blood groups to the problem of racial classification.

First, we note the blood groups occurring in nonhuman primates. They demonstrate remarkable similarities to those present in man. Their distribution is of some assistance in helping to understand the nature of the factors involved in the distribution of blood groups among human populations.

Secondly, we observe the incidence of blood types (the frequency with which a particular type occurs in a given population) among human populations throughout the world. We know that no human group is homogeneous for a particular blood type; that is, all types are represented in all populations. However, we have found that single blood types appear in highly varied percentages. Ottenberg was one of the first to undertake a racial classification based on blood groups according to geographic distribution. Such a classification system would be supremely useful for numerous reasons. First, blood type is inheritable and has been found to occur in accordance with Mendelian laws; secondly, blood type is not influenced by environmental factors (climate, disease, diet, etc.). Further, blood types may be reliably determined without gradation from one type to another. In other words, an individual's blood type may be determined without subjective measurement. It is stable, remaining as it is throughout the lifetime of the person regardless of external factors.

But a racial classification is not built on one trait alone. The criterion is a valid one; it awaits refinement and careful application, in collaboration with other significant criteria in order to contribute to our knowledge of mankind's races.

A further point regarding the investigation of blood groups: there are indications that persons belonging to different blood groups may vary substantially in their susceptibility to certain diseases. For example, individuals with Type A blood demonstrate a higher incidence of bronchial pneumonia, stomach cancer, and other illnesses, while those with Type O are seemingly susceptible to duodenal, gastric, and peptic ulcers. Again, however, our figures are not conclusive. Further investigation, with an ever increasing accumulation of reliable blood classifications, will be required before we are able to generalize regarding blood type and disease.

There are numerous other racial criteria in use today and under investigation. The Mongolian spot, for instance, is found in frequency varying with geographical location. The PTC test (for Phenylthiocarbamide) has gained increasing favor among investigators. PTC—as it is understandably better known—is a white crystalline powder. Some people (tasters) can taste it, while others (nontasters) cannot. Alternate gene forms are involved in the transmission of the ability to taste PTC: T (dominant for tasting) and t (recessive for nontasting). There are obvious population differences: of a group of Japanese tested, over ninety per cent had the ability to taste the substance, as compared with fifty per cent of the Australian aborigine sample and almost one hundred per cent of American Indians tested. This is all very interesting, since tasting is not a selective factor. Our knowledge, however, is not sufficient to reconstruct historical relationships on this basis.

Before progressing to a racial taxonomy, we would do well to consider race and intelligence. For a long time, hereditary and racial differences in intellectual capacity have been accepted as truths. Much of this erroneous acceptance has been based upon the standard intelligence tests in use today. It is quite clear that such tests *do not* measure inherent gene-determined potentialities, as intelligence tests are never culture-free. They measure in relation to a particular cultural background, causing those individuals with language skills and acquired knowledge (largely urban individuals) to score higher than those who lack these advantages. The I.Q. tests, then, reflect the level of motivation, coupled with socioeconomic background, rather than inherent ability. This is not to say that such tests are invalid; they can and do record performance and experience in school and are useful in assessing progress made scholastically. They must not, however, be used to demonstrate inferiority of a given race.

Actually, racial differences in measured intelligence have been neither proved nor disproved. There are differences, but, like stature, these differences do not necessarily indicate the maximum level of intellectual capacity in the absence of standard or controlled conditions.

In the following chapter, we will attempt to devise a racial classification based upon the criteria we have discussed here, keeping in mind that such a classification is temporary, subject to revision as our present stockpile of knowledge grows through present and future investigations.

Suggested Readings

Montagu, M. F. Ashley
    1960. *A Handbook of Anthropometry.* Springfield, Ill.: Charles C Thomas.

Mourant, A. E., A. C. Kopec and K. Domaniewska-Sobczak
    1958. *The ABO Blood Groups: comprehensive tables and maps of world distribution.* Oxford: Blackwell Scientific Publs.

Race, R. R. and Ruth Sanger
    1958. *Blood Groups in Man* (3d ed.). Springfield, Ill.: Charles C Thomas.

Wiener, A. S. and I. B. Wexler
    1958. *Heredity of the Blood Groups.* New York: Grune & Stratton.

RACE
chapter
12

Until quite recent times, the study of race in man consisted primarily of detailed descriptions of diverse human populations, composed strictly for comparative purposes. Recently, however, the investigation of different human groups through measurement, description, and photography has become an integral part of the study of evolution. Particular attention is now paid to the evolutionary mechanisms operating in the formation of human races.

As we learned more about the human populations present during Pleistocene times, we began to extend our studies backward in time, adding another dimension to our work. Now we have seen that race relates to human variations, that isolating a particular race involves a recognition of biological differences among a number of populations. Numerous racial classifications have been devised, distinguishing from two to over a hundred distinct races. Naturally, this disparity in figures results from an overly elastic application of the term *race,* with some investigators utilizing racial criteria in a different manner from others.

The most practical approach to racial investigation was devised by Garn [1] and involves the consideration of three basic population groupings:

1. *Geographical races,* groups of racial populations isolated from other such groups by major geographic barriers;

2. *Local races,* groups existing within geographical races but separated from other local races by distance, geographic barriers, or cultural factors;

3. *Micro-races,* groups within local races which are distinguished from other micro-races through the recognition of regional differences.

Geographical races, of course, make up the largest of the three groupings and actually encompass the other two. We refer to the Australian people, for example, or to the people of South America in pre-Columbian time. Within the geographical designation, individual populations resemble each other more or less, but intrapopulation differences are still notable; we might speak of the South American peoples but point to individual populations whose members tend to be tall, for instance, or short. Basically, a geographical race is a collection of populations whose similarities are due to long-continued confinement within fixed geographical limits.

Local races correspond more closely to what we think of as breeding populations. These are isolated within geographical races, as we have seen, by a number of factors. Among African peoples, for example, the Bushmen of South Africa are notably different from the Masai of Kenya; distance keeps them apart. And Eskimo groups, while belonging to a single geographical race, cannot easily mate with members of other Eskimo groups; territorial limits are typically defined, and breeding occurs between groups geographically close or, usually, is confined to the local race itself. Actually, because of this confinement, the local races exist as independent evolutionary units, as there is little or no gene exchange in the absence of outbreeding.

Garn points out that in densely populated areas, local races may not be demonstrable, yet biological distance may maintain regional differentiation. Such differences account for micro-races. Even in large cities, regional differences are apparent, due in part to ancient settlement and mating patterns. With millions

[1] Garn, Stanley M. *Human Races* (2d ed.). Springfield: Charles C Thomas, 1962.

of potential mates, the male tends to choose one near at hand —the "girl next door," so to speak—and the denser the population, the more likely is this to be the case.

What causes race? A number of genetic mechanisms to explain population differentiation have been noted in operation, both in time and in space. The most obvious are:

1. *Mutation:* As we have seen, mutation is *a spontaneous change in genetic material that can be transmitted to succeeding generations.* In man, most mutations have been detrimental, the reason being that natural selection operates to select and propagate the best-suited or most fit, and the organ which changes through mutation has already undergone changes through time which make it the best fit. However, in a period of changing environment or new opportunities, an occasional mutation may be advantageous and thus take hold. Then the process of change begins. Scientists estimate human mutation rates as lying somewhere between five and fifty per cent per one million births. High radioactivity has most probably increased our mutation rate. Advantageous mutation, of course, operates most successfully within a small population.

2. *Natural selection:* This evolutionary mechanism is clearly important in modifying whole species and higher taxonomic groups. For example, a faster species of antelope may have a better chance to survive than slower types. All of the climatic forces we see around us are potential selective agents bringing about, through genetic adaptation, differentiation between races. Among the most obvious are the abundance or scarcity of food and disease, which favors those with superior immunity.

An example of natural selection in man is seen in *sickle-cell anemia,* a serious anemia usually fatal before maturity of the afflicted individual. The condition arises with destruction of the red cells and can be diagnosed microscopically through the examination of the red corpuscles, which typically assume a sickle shape, similar to a holly leaf. Investigators have noted a Negroid distribution of this disease. The distribution in Africa is highly variable (from zero to forty per cent), a phenomenon difficult to understand. Since the disease is usually lethal, the high incidence noted among certain Negroid groups must have some selective advantage. Investigators found that the high incidence of sicklemia corresponds with areas where malaria is most common. Apparently, heterozygous individuals (those with genes both for normal and for sickling corpuscles) are more immune to malaria than are homozygous normals. This, then, is a case of double selection: against homozygous sicklers (doomed to serious anemia and likely death) and against homozygous normals (lacking immunity to malaria). The biological price of maintaining a heterozygote population is the birth of both homozygotes (normal and sicklers) with each generation.

3. *Genetic drift: the accidental increase or decrease in particular gene frequencies.* As we have seen, this phenomenon results from chance fluctuations in the breeding structure of small populations. The occurrence of genetic drift is of particular interest to investigators, because the early human populations must have been small in size and number. Skeletal remains from the Pleistocene suggest that a typical population seldom numbered more than fifty individuals.

4. *Isolation:* We know that mating is selective; that is, there is a definite tendency for members of subgroups to mate among themselves, isolating themselves genetically from other subgroups and maintaining stable gene pools. This isolation may arise from geographic considerations or from existing physical differences; certain people look different, and, as opposites do not usually attract, an individual searches for a mate whose differences are minute. Sexual selection, too, plays a role here; there are preferred standards of beauty in each population. And social selection cannot be overlooked: there are cultural regulations, *customs,* which act to enforce particular breeding patterns within groups.

All of these mechanisms work together on a single polytypic species like man. Certainly they were functioning when human populations were just beginning to develop, at the time when races were beginning to form.

A Racial Taxonomy

We have considered a number of racial criteria and have examined a few of the evolutionary mechanisms which operate to maintain them. The next logical step is to incorporate our criteria into a taxonomy for man, a listing of the larger and smaller groups among humans. For living man, there is but one species and, within the species, about nine geographical races: Amerindian, Polynesian, Micronesian, Melanesian-Papuan, Australian, Asiatic, Indian, European, and African. In each case, geographical barriers set off these race collections. But there are also local races, constituting a problem because there are so many of them; and there are numerous local races which have not as yet been completely identified.

But how many races are there? Some authorities prefer to speak of physical stocks, defining only *Negroid* (those peoples primarily from Africa south of the Sahara), *Caucasoid* (those from Northern Africa and Europe), and *Mongoloid* (the Asiatic peoples). Others recognize dozens of racial groups. Depending upon the investigator and his criteria, there may be as few as three races or as many as a hundred or more. The present authors have chosen to accept in large part those races identified by Garn. In enumerating these, we will keep in mind that until there is universal agreement on racial criteria and some means is found to weigh their importance relatively, identification of races is largely a matter of personal opinion. It would be wise to remember, also, as we list the following geographical races, that there is very considerable diversity within each.

AMERINDIAN GEOGRAPHICAL RACE

Consisting of a large number of local populations and ranging from Alaska, Northern Canada, and Labrador to the southernmost tip of South America. Populations within the Amerindian grouping are typically small, usually marginal, hunting-and-gathering or semiagricultural peoples. Genetic isolation is frequently complete, with little or no interbreeding among separate local groups.

Typically, the Amerindian populations demonstrate a high incidence of Group O blood, with a low incidence of Group A and an almost complete absence of Type B. In morphology, the members of this geographical race exhibit straight, coarse hair, although there are exceptions in South America, where wavy hair is the rule. Beard and body hair are sparse to absent, with the exception of the North American Piute. Eyes are dark brown, hair black to dark brown, with some reddish tints in

South America. Skin color is yellow-brown to reddish brown or dark brown. Faces tend to be wide, with projecting malars (cheekbones) and alveolar prognathism (forward protrusion of the jaws). The epicanthic fold (a small fold of skin sometimes covering the inner corner of the eye) is common.

Remember: these are trait averages, with many exceptions. For example, some South American populations range in skin color from almost white to chocolate brown. Reports of "white Indians" in Latin America, however, are erroneous; these actually represent cases of endemic partial albinism, as among the San Blas Indians of Darien.

POLYNESIAN GEOGRAPHICAL RACE

Occupying a vast territory in the Pacific from New Zealand to the Hawaiian and Easter Islands. Many now uninhabited islands bear traces of earlier seafaring local races.

Members reflect serology high in A and O types of blood. Morphologically, individuals tend to have wavy head hair, with beard and body hair sparse to absent. Hair is black, with some reddish tints occurring. Skin follows the brunette pattern, white to brown. Eyes are brown, medium to dark. There is often a slight inner epicanthic fold. Faces are usually wide, long, and heavy. In stature, the Polynesians are tall, the male averaging 5'9".

MICRONESIAN GEOGRAPHICAL RACE

Occupying a series of small islands in the Pacific from Ulithi and Palau Islands (near Guam) to the Marshall and Gilbert Islands. There is a high incidence of Type A blood. Morphologically, individuals have wavy hair, sometimes frizzy, and are dark brown in skin color. In many features, they are similar to the Polynesians, but Asiatic features are more numerous and more easily demonstrated. Stature is short rather than tall.

MELANESIAN-PAPUAN GEOGRAPHICAL RACE

Occupying the region known as Melanesia and beyond. Little was known about this population until World War II. There is a high incidence of Type B blood. Skulls are robust. Hair occurs in curls, twists, and frizzes, often termed "woolly." Skin color is dark brown to black. The individuals of this area are often referred to as the "Pacific Negroids."

AUSTRALIAN GEOGRAPHICAL RACE

Constituting a series of local races clearly related to the now extinct Tasmanians. There is a low incidence of Type B blood, unlike the Melanesians, with whom they are sometimes erroneously grouped. Wavy hair is the rule; curly hair occurs occasionally, but straight hair is unknown. Beard and body hair are abundant. Hair is dark brown with reddish tints. Skin color is yellow-brown to chocolate brown, eyes brown, medium to dark. The head is typically narrow, with pronounced facial prognathism and large teeth.

ASIATIC GEOGRAPHICAL RACE

Occupying continental Asia and into Japan, and in the Philippines, Sumatra, Borneo and Celebes islands. Here is an excellent example of the gross differences which can be noted among geographical races; the Asiatics include both the short, infantile peoples of Indonesia and the tall, rugged populations of Northern China.

Type B blood is frequent. Hair is straight and coarse, with body hair and beard sparse. Hair, skin, and eyes are brown. The epicanthic fold is common. Faces are broad with fat-padded malars. There are at least one hundred local races noted, the most recognizable being the Tungus, Chinese, Japanese, Burmese, Javanese, and the Ainu, legendary "hairy people" of Northern Japan, who are biologically and culturally isolated from their neighbors to a very great extent.

INDIAN GEOGRAPHICAL RACE

Extending from the High Himalayas to the Indian Ocean. This group is also broken up into a number of local races with diverse languages and religions. Type B blood is common, and Rh negative is low in incidence, these two facts separating the Indians from the European grouping and making them appear to be more closely related to the Asiatic grouping. Morphologically, the Indians are very similar to the Europeans, but there are differences: skin color is darker, and body build is more linear.

EUROPEAN GEOGRAPHICAL RACE

Comprises a collection of local races and micro-races inhabiting (during Pre-Columbian times) Europe, Western Asia, the Middle East, and Africa north of the Sahara.

Typically, groups are high in Rh negative, a characteristic unique in man so far as population averages are concerned. Males tend to be hirsute, with a tendency toward balding. Pigmentation varies: skin is pale white or pink to dark brown, hair blond to dark brown, and eyes blue to dark brown. Hair is wavy or straight. The nose is typically high and narrow.

There are numerous local races involved—for example, the Lapps, fishermen and herders of West Russia, Finland, Sweden, and Norway. These people are characterized by small stature, fragile body build, brachycephalic skulls, and small teeth.

AFRICAN GEOGRAPHICAL RACE

Constitutes a collection of local races and micro-races, all indigenous to Africa south of the Sahara Desert. As we have noted, these populations (Negroid) show a high incidence of sickle-cell anemia. Hair form is woolly or frizzy, while beard and body hair are sparse. Heavy pigmentation is the rule; hair is black, skin and eyes dark brown to black. The head is typically narrow, the face short. The nose is wide, and facial prognathism is common. There is much variation between local races, especially in regard to stature. For example, included in this single geographical grouping are the Pygmies of the Ituri Rain Forest. For comparative purposes, we note too the Bushmen-Hottentot groups, which represent aboriginal inhabitants of South Africa. These exhibit less pigmentation than the other groups but combine this lighter skin color with other, more typical features—peppercorn hair, for example, the hair form characterized by growth in spiral tufts. Also characteristic of this local race is *steatopygia*, gluteal fat deposits on the buttocks, most extremely developed in the female.

In addition to these nine basic groupings, we have hybrid populations of recent origin. The American Negro represents an African-European cross, and the Neo-Hawaiian peoples demonstrate a complex of characters associated with groups from northwest and southern Europe, Polynesia, China, Japan, and the Philippines. And, of course, there are local races, as noted in a few examples above, as well as micro-races. These subgroups number into the thousands and are recognized in racial classification systems only when racial criteria validate their isolation from other subgroups. Our purpose here is not to itemize literally thousands of subgroups but to indicate the presence of human differentiation and those factors which induce such variation.

Suggested Readings

Boyd, W. C.
    1966. Genetics and the races of man. *In:* Thomas W. McKern (ed.), *Readings in Physical Anthropology*, pp. 168–73. Englewood Cliffs, N.J.: Prentice-Hall, Inc.

Garn, Stanley M. (ed.)
    1960. *Readings on Race*. Springfield: Charles C Thomas.

    1962. *Human Races* (2d ed.). Springfield: Charles C Thomas.

Glass, B., M. S. Sacks, E. F. John, and C. Hess
    1952. Genetic drift in a religious isolate. *Amer. Naturalist*, 86:145–59.

Klineberg, O.
    1966. Race differences: the present position of the problem. *In:* Thomas W. McKern (ed.), *Readings in Physical Anthropology*. Englewood Cliffs, N.J.: Prentice-Hall, Inc.

ANTHROPOLOGY: TODAY AND TOMORROW

chapter
13

We have seen in the preceding pages numerous problems with which anthropology is concerned. The physical anthropologist works within this framework. In order to derive maximum knowledge, however, he does not normally concern himself in detail with the totality of the subject, although man as a complex entity is never far from his mind. Generally, he chooses to *specialize,* to focus his attention primarily upon one segment of the overall problem and research intensively in order to know all he can about a single problem area.

In days past, he might have chosen race, or fossil history, or reproduction for his specialized inquiry. Today, even such subproblems are unmanageable because of the bulky accumulation of knowledge with which he must deal and the myriad questions that knowledge induces. The physical anthropologist, then, will concentrate upon an even more specialized aspect of that subproblem—the relationship of climate and race, for example, or the incidence of sickle-cell anemia in a number of populations. Thus there are men who devote their entire lives to the study of the most minute influences upon human development. It is only in this way that the science as a whole can advance.

But what does it all mean? How are the apparent minutiae resolved into a larger whole? And after all the facts are in, the interpretations made, the results tabulated, toward what ends is this knowledge applied? Toward what goals are the men in the laboratories and in the field working?

The Continued Refinement of Research Tools

Often, scientific advances are turned immediately back into investigation, much in the same way that a business corporation reinvests its profits into the next year's operations. The human osteologist, for example, utilizes techniques derived in the nineteenth century in his twentieth-century investigation of human skeletal material, giving us additional information on past and present populations. The experts concerned with fossil material apply the principles of taxonomy to new fossil finds, revising that taxonomy when necessary, obtaining even more knowledge about the past and enhancing the very taxonomic system which he utilizes in research. The racial anthropologist applies his methodology toward a still better understanding of race.

Outside the Laboratory

At the same time, however, these men seek a practical application of their tools to solve present-day problems. The osteologist may be called upon to use his skills in identifying victims of war, disaster, or accident. He may act in consultation with local legal agencies to related unidentified dead with known missing persons. If he has specialized in dermatoglyphics, he sees his research in use throughout the world in the fingerprint files now so commonly used in identification of human individuals.

The anthropologist who has concerned himself with race may

now be called upon to clarify problems relating to race. He may work closely with social agencies and with the behavioral scientists toward the alleviation of racial problems and prejudices. Or he may be asked to ascertain the probable parentage of a child available for adoption.

The *paidologist* (a specialist in anthropometry concerned with the nature, growth, and development of children) is in frequent demand as we seek to provide our young with the best possible conditions for development, both physical and social. The medical anthropologist may be called upon to investigate (and thus alleviate) the problems of disease. For example, he may identify the causes of particular diseases among distinct urban populations by studying their diet or health patterns, as seen in the work of numerous experts who have focused upon such transient groups as the Mexican-American crop workers.

In the field of space exploration, the data made available through physical anthropology has seen new and exciting application. Almost every facet of an astronaut's existence is related in some manner to studies in physical anthropology, and typical areas of investigation receiving particular emphasis may include pathology, genetics, biological systems in space conditions, effects of space on biological rhythms and orientation, and the anthropometrics of different populations at any given time. On a more earthly level, applied physical anthropology is reflected in human engineering at every turn: the coat you wear was manufactured in your size because anthropometry made available to the clothing industry a standard of population measurements. The chair upon which you sit was designed to seat an "average" individual: average in your time and in your country.

Twentieth-Century Trends

It has been said that the history of science exhibits a sustained and orderly progression from the past to the present and that it is the only history that does so. As far as the history of physical anthropology is concerned, we can accord this assumption some measure of truth. Current theoretical and technological aspects of physical anthropology stand as intricately conceived and finely constructed products of a sustained developmental process. We have said, of course, that physical anthropology—as it is termed today—is a recent science. But studies within its proper province date back to the time of the early Greeks. Medical treatment, based on wide knowledge of human anatomy, dates from ancient Egypt, more than a thousand years before Hippocrates. And even earlier man pondered his own origins.

At the same time, the history of physical anthropology belongs as much (or more!) to the twentieth century as it does to the past, both qualitatively and quantitatively. The science has experienced unbelievable growth and expansion in recent years. While the methods and theories of what is now known as physical anthropology proceeded in a continuing progression from the time of Greece until 1900, it has been during the present century that its establishment as a versatile science has been most fully realized.

The question arises whether it is possible to appraise objectively the history of anthropology in the twentieth century, for the nearness of events chronologically may tend to distort their true significance as elements of history. Such an argument, while logical, must be subject to extensive qualification. Certainly general assumptions can be legitimately made concerning most of the aspects of modern physical anthropology.

Dr. Juan Comas and numerous others have warned against the danger of separating the modern science into different schools of thought: "pure" and "applied." This remains an important consideration, despite the fact that physical anthropology has grown to such an extent that it includes not only theoretical problems in the realm of scientific research but also numerous areas of practical application. But man *is* practical; we tend to believe that a science, in order to justify its own existence, must in some way be applied to the needs of man. The future of the science depends on both pure research and the application of knowledge to benefit present mankind.

Perhaps the most specific contribution to the modern era of science by physical anthropology has been the explanation that, while there may be meaningful biological differences between separate groups of people, the concept of race—as judged solely by outwardly visible features—is at best an untrustworthy one. In this time of racial conflict and uncertainty, this is no small contribution. But it is not the single gift made by the science to mankind.

In recent years, physical anthropology has tended toward greater experimentation and is increasingly influenced by modern genetic theory. In the United States, this is most certainly true. In other areas of the world, specialized interests have marked a tremendous growth in all aspects of the science. Population analyses have become increasingly useful, particularly in India. British contributions in recent years have made possible expansion of knowledge in such fields as human evolution, statistical analysis, and constitutional anthropology. From Italy, we have important data from the population geneticists. A pronounced influence by the Nazi regime has stultified German efforts in the field, but recent investigations indicate a resurgence of the brilliant scientific experimentation so characteristic of that country in the past.

There are too many aspects of physical anthropology to even attempt an analysis of specific trends, although the few noted above are so outstanding that they come quickly to mind. What is of paramount importance is that while physical anthropology has received many applications in the modern world, it remains a basic science, comprising theoretical concepts, scientific methods, and local systems of practical application. To view physical anthropology in any other manner would be to diminish its ultimate influence and contributions to mankind.

Future Man

But what of modern man? Certainly all of us have wondered from time to time about the future development of our species, from both a cultural and a biological viewpoint. It is interesting to speculate on such things as future cities, future foods, and—most especially—what man will look like in a million years or so, if he's still around.

Most of these speculations are purely a matter of turning

science to fun-making, with an educated guess here and there, as evidenced by comic strips and the science fiction novels so much a part of our culture. There seem to be two general schools of thought regarding the future development of man: the "superman" school and the "brainy" school.

The "superman" school is based upon a belief in physical perfection. Advocates foresee no radical change in morphology; they believe man will look pretty much as he does today except that evolution will operate on what man has to make it better and more functional. Such enhanced faculties as enormous strength and X-ray vision are predicted.

The "brainy" school, on the other hand, holds that the essence of man is his brain, and therefore evolution will concentrate on this area, more or less ignoring the rest. According to this view, there will be great morphological change: huge, bald heads, reduced bodies, spindly little legs.

Both schools of thought are products of overworked imaginations, but both are based on fragments of evidence gleaned from man's evolutionary past. There are those who predict that a million years hence, man will be anything that the geneticists desire, with changes induced through exposure of genes to nuclear rays or chemicals. As long as we are dreaming, we might wish for powerful brains, with the accompanying increase in leisure time. But let's consider future possibilities, looking first at what we've been given to work with.

The human body is a complex and intricate mechanism, the best evolution has yet produced. Yet it has a great many weaknesses. Looking at man as a machine, we see such a hodgepodge, such a great accumulation of adaptations and revisions, that the real wonder rests in the fact that we get along as well as we do. Most of our weaknesses are related to upright posture; these flaws represent imperfect adaptations to a completely new posture. We have achieved our orthograde posture at a high price.

First, the skeletal structure of a four-legged animal is a walking bridge. Upended, as we are, that structure is in terrific imbalance. The upright structure has had to accommodate itself somehow to the new vertical stance bearing various stresses. The curves seen dorsally in the human body are supposed to compensate for the numerous weight and stress problems.

At birth, the human spine curls in a simple ancestral arch. At about four months of age, a baby holds his head upright, causing a forward curve in the neck region. At one year, the child stands, assuming a forward curve in his lower trunk. Quite literally, as we grow, we twist our backbones into adult shape to compensate for weight stresses upon the upright posture. And numerous changes are required. The vertebrae have been modified in form, permitting movement. But such a condition weakens the backbone, and heavy lifting or sudden stress may cause lower vertebrae to slip backward or forward, producing pain. The vertebrae are prone to arthritis. An intervertebral disc may be squeezed out due to a crushing weight, and sacroiliac articulation often causes discomfort. You might say that the phrase "Oh, my aching back!" has an evolutionary significance. With upright posture, the sacrum has broadened and is lower, now encroaching upon the pelvic cavity and narrowing the birth canal, leading to obstetrical problems. The ilium (hip bone) is shortened and broadened, lengthening the waist.

The viscera are unchanged and must continue to operate, the same old structures in a new position. Increased weight from upright stance may lead to herniation, both common and painful. The heart, now about four feet above ground, must overcome the extra gravitational pull, resulting in sluggish circulation in the extremities and such undesirable but human problems as varicose veins and hemorrhoids (congestion of veins at the end of the intestine).

Also, our two-legged posture places too great a burden on our feet, which have changed but not enough. We are plagued by fallen arches, bunions, and calluses. And our eyes were never constructed for the strains we place upon them. Glasses or contact lenses are normal and necessary pieces of equipment for most of us.

Sounds pretty bad, doesn't it? But it is what we have been given to work with. At least, it represents the present stage in the evolutionary development of man. Where do we go from here? Is there any evidence that might suggest future developmental trends?

Our brains are *not* becoming larger, but rounder, a trend seemingly entrenched sufficiently to suggest continuation. As brains become more round, faces shrink. And there is evidence for decreased face size, bone for bone. Future possibilities include higher noses, more pointed chins, and a general shrinking backward of the human face.

As far as the teeth go, we seem to be losing them. The first mammals had 66 teeth, while modern mammals have only 44; the early primates counted 36 teeth, and today man has 32. There is seldom room in the human jaw for the growth of a third molar, and most of us have these removed as they appear. Numerous individuals are born with a congenitally absent third molar. Quite possibly more and more of us will be so favored.

What about the little toes? Anthropologists have been predicting their decline and disappearance for years. And we may lose them. They are almost vestigial, but, then again, we still have many vestigial organs. One thing is certain: some of us are losing our hair. Baldness is on the increase. The trait for baldness is sex-linked, appearing therefore more often in the male. Also, it is a trend apparent only among Caucasoids at present.

Speculation is fun, so long as we remember that it *is* speculation. We will most probably look much as we do today for a good long time. Changes will be small and slow to show phenotypically. As we become more and more able to control our own genetic destiny through laboratory techniques, we will select to preserve and enhance the features we prize, discarding those which trouble us. Hopefully, we will keep the human brain the way it is, using that much to better advantage and making more of its total potential. Doubtless, there will be improved musculature, with stronger weight-bearing areas. Perhaps—though it is not likely—we will all be of one color; if not, perhaps we will learn that color is not all-important.

This is physical anthropology, in brief outline. We have touched the surface, all we can do in one volume. If we have attempted to make a single point, it has been to emphasize the fact that man's biological past, present, and future are not easily or simply understood. But the science of man is young, and this means that the many questions we are unable to answer today will be answered, sometime, tomorrow.

Suggested Readings

Rostand, J.
    1959. *Can Man Be Modified?* New York: Basic Books.

Stern, C.
    1966. Man's genetic future. *In:* Thomas W. McKern (ed.), *Readings in Physical Anthropology,* pp. 194–98. Englewood Cliffs, N.J.: Prentice-Hall, Inc.

INDEX

A

Abbevillian, 107–9
ABO Blood System, 172–75
Acheulian, 94, 108, 109, 112
Adapis, 66
Adaptation, 25, 60, 64
Afalou, 98
Albinism, 158, 184
Alleles, 157, 158
Allosomes, 156
Amphipithecus, 67
Anagale, 66
Analogous:
  chromosomes, 153
  organs, 12–13
Anaptomorphidae, 67
Anatomy, comparative, 6, 34–35
Anemia, sickle-cell, 181–82, 189
Animalia, characteristics of, 10, 13–14
Anthropoidea, characteristics of, 15–16
Anthropometry, 5
  in race studies, 167–69

Anyathian, 111
Archeology, 4
Archeomagnetism, 54
Art, Upper Paleolithic, 115–16
Artifact, 102 (*see also* Cultural prehistory)
Aterian, 118
Atlanthropus mauritanicus, 111
Aurignacian, 115–16
Australoid, 99
Australopithecus, 79–82, 84, 88, 99, 110
  africanus, 80–81, 82, 110
  robustus, 80–81

B

Baboon, 131–34
Blood types, 172–75 (*see also* Serology)
Bone tools, 106 (*see also* Osteodontokeratic)
Boskop, 98
Brachiation, 63, 134

Brain, primate evolution of, 62–63
Bramapithecus, 71
Broca, P., 5
Broken Hill, 89, 92, 113
Broom, R., 79, 84
Buckland, D., 22

C

Capsian, 118
Carbon-14, 54–55, 56, 121, 122, 123
Carpenter, C. R., 129, 134
Catastrophism, 22
Caucasoid, 99, 183
Ceboidea, 16, 129–31, 133
Cebupithecia, 72
Cephalic index, 168–69
Cercopithecoidea, 16, 131–34
Chancelade, 98, 99, 117
Chellean, 85, 107, 111
Chelles-Acheul, 110, 113
Chimpanzee, 138–41
Choanichthyes, 49
Chopper-chopping tools, 111
Chordata, characteristics of, 14
Choukoutien, 85, 98
Choukoutienian, 111
Chromosome, 27, 149, 151, 152, 153, 155, 156, 157, 159
Cingulum, 61, 62
Clactonian, 108, 112
Classification (*see* Taxonomy)
Clovis, 120
Color blindness, 160
Core tool, 107
Cranial capacity (*see* Brain, primate evolution of)
Cro Magnon, 98, 99, 115
Crossopterygians, 49
Cultural prehistory, 102–23
Cuvier, B. G., 22

D

Dart, R., 79, 110
Darwin, C., 22–25, 30–31, 33
Dating methods (*see* Geochronology)
Dendrochronology, 53–54
Dental formula, 16–17, 61
Diastema, 71
Diploid, 153
DNA, 147, 148, 161, 162
Dominance, behavioral, 130, 132, 135, 137, 139
Dominance, hereditary, 156–58
Double selection, 182
Dryopithecus, 69, 70

E

Ehringsdorf, 93
Embryology, 6, 35–37
Epicanthic fold, 171, 184, 185
Erect posture (*see* Orthograde)
Erthroblastosis fetalis, 174
Ethnography, 4
Ethnology, 4
Eutheria, 15, 39, 61

F

Flake production, 106
Flake tool, 107
Fluorine analysis, 53, 123
Folsom, 122
Fontechevade, 95, 112
Foramen magnum, 63, 67, 79
Fossilization, 41, 48
Fossil primates, 58–73
Fouresmith, 113, 118

G

Garn, S., 180, 183
Gene, 147, 148, 157, 158, 159, 160, 161, 162
    lethal, 161
Gene pool, 162, 182
Genetic drift, 163, 182
Genetics, 42, 145–63 (see also Heredity)
Genotype, 157–58, 167
Geochronology, 52–57
    absolute, 54–55
    relative, 52–53
Geographic determinism, 39
Geography, 37–39
Gibbon, 134–36
Gigantopithecus, 69, 70
Goodall, J., 138, 139, 140
Gorilla, 136–38
Grimaldi, 98, 99, 116

H

Haploid, 153
Heidelberg, 94, 95
Hemophilia, 160
Heredity, 145–63
Heterodonty, 61
Heterozygous, 157, 158, 182
Hominidae, taxonomic characteristics of, 17
    differentiation from Pongidae, 78, 79
Hominoidea, taxonomic characteristics of, 16–17
Homo erectus, 84–88, 89, 94, 96, 99, 111
Homo habilis, 81, 84, 110
Homologous:
    chromosomes, 153, 157
    organs, 12–13
Homo sapiens neanderthalensis, 88–94, 96, 98, 112–13, 114, 119

Homo sapiens sapiens, 93, 95, 96, 98–99, 118
Homozygous, 157, 158, 160, 161
Homunculus, 72
Hotu, 98
Howler monkey, 129–31
Hurzeler, Johannes, 71
Hybridization, 163, 187

I

Isolation, 37, 39, 182, 183

K

Keilor, 98, 99
Kohler, W., 128
Krapina, 93

L

La Chapelle, 89, 93
Lamarck, J., 25
La Quina, 93
Law of Independent Assortment, 30
Law of Segregation, 28
    schematic representation, 29
Law of Superposition, 46
    schematic representation, 47
Leakey, L. S. B., 70, 81, 84, 85
Levalloisian, 109, 112, 113, 118 (see also Levalloiso-Mousterian)
Levalloiso-Mousterian, 113, 118
Limnopithecus, 68
Linguistics, 4
Linnaeus, C., 10, 11
Lyell, C., 23

M

Magdalenian, 116–17
Makapansgat, 80
Malthus, T. R., 23
Mammalia, characteristics of, 14–15
Man-apes (*see Australopithecus*)
Meganthropus paleojavanicus, 88
Meiosis, 152–53, 154
Melanin, 169, 170
Mendel, Gregor, 26–30, 156, 157
Mendelian population, 162
Metatheria, 15, 39
Midland, 22
Mitosis, 148–52
Mongoloid, 99, 171, 183
Mongoloid spot, 175
Monophyletic, 99
Montmaurin, 96
Mt. Carmel, 93
Mousterian, 112, 114–15
Mutation, 148, 160–62, 171, 181

N

Natural selection, 23, 181
Neanderthal (*see Homo sapiens neanderthalensis*)
Negroid, 99, 183, 186
New World prehistory, 119–23
Notharctus, 66

O

Obercassel, 117
Oldoway, 98 (*see also* Olduvai)
Olduvai, 81 (*see also* Oldoway)
Oligopithecus, 68
Oogenesis, 153
Orang-utan, 136
Ordosian, 119
Oreopithecus, 71
Orthogenesis, 59–60
Orthograde, 63, 103, 194–95
Osteodontokeratic, 110
Osteology, 5

P

Paleoanthropology, 5
Paleo-Indian, 120 (*see also* New World prehistory)
Paleolithic, 106
　Lower, 107–11
　Middle, 111–13
　Upper, 114–18
Paleontology, 41
Pantotheria, 61
Parapithecus, 68
Parthenogenesis, 146
Patjitanian, 111
Perigordian, 115
Petrifaction, 48
Phenotype, 157–58, 163
Phenylthiocarbamide, 175–76
Pithecanthropus erectus (*see Homo erectus*)
Placenta, 15, 174
Plesiadapidae, 66
Pliopithecus, 68
Pollen analysis, 53
Polyphyletic, 99
Pongidae, 17, 134–43 (*see also* Fossil primates)
Potassium-argon, 55, 56
Pre-Chelles-Acheul, 84, 110
Predmost, 98
Pre-Soan, 111
Primates:
　fossil, 58–73
　living, 125–29
　taxonomic characteristics of, 15
Primatology, 5, 125–43 (*see also* Primates)
Proconsul, 69, 70
Pronograde, 63, 103, 194–95
Propliopithecus, 68

Prosimii, taxonomic characteristics of, 15–16
Prototheria, 15

R

Race, 164–77, 179–87, 190–91
 defined, 166
 and intelligence, 176
Ramapithecus, 69, 70–71
Reduction division, 153, 154
Reproduction, 146, 147
Reynolds, V., 138, 141
Rh factor, 174
Rhodesian, 113
RNA, 147
Rooneyia viejaensis, 67–68

S

Saldanha, 89
Sandia, 120
Sangoan, 113, 118
Schaffhausen, Hermann, 88
Schaller, G., 136
Schoetensack, O., 94
Sebilian, 118
Serology, 6, 39–41 (see also ABO Blood System)
 in human races, 172–75
 primate, 40
 type chart, 173
Sex determination, 153–56
Sex-limited, 159
Sex linkage, 158–60
Shanidar, 89, 93
Shovel-shaped incisor, 171
Sinanthropus pekinensis (see *Homo erectus*)
Sivapithecus, 69
Skhul, 89, 93
Skin color, 169–70
Society of Anthropology, 5
Solutrean, 116, 117
Somatology, 5
Speciation, 145
Species, 17
Spermatogenesis, 152
Spy, 93
Steatopygia, 186
Steinheim, 94–95, 96
Sterkfontein, 80
Stillbay, 118
Stone tools, manufacture of, 104–6
Subspecies, 18
Swanscombe, 94, 96, 109
Synapsis, 152
Systematics (see Taxonomy)

T

Tarsiidae, 67
Tarsiiforme, 66
Taungs, 80
Taxonomy, 9–19, 75–77, 190
 definition, 9
 phylogenetic, 11–12
 Polytypic, 165
 typological, 11
Tayacian, 112
Telanthropus capensis, 81, 84
Tepexpan, 122
Trilobates, 49

U

Ussher, Archbishop, 22

V

Vallois, H., 168
Varve analysis, 54
Vertebrata, taxonomic characteristics of, 14
Vèrtesszöllös, 85
Viviparous birth, 14, 51

W

Wadjak, 98, 99
Wallace, A., 23
Wallace's Line, 39
Weissmann, A., 26

X

Xenopithecus, 69
X-linked inheritance *(see* Sex linkage)

Y

Y-5 dentition, 69–70
Y-linked inheritance *(see* Sex linkage)

Z

Zinjanthropus boisei, 80, 110
Zuckerman, S., 126, 131, 132
Zygote, 153